ESSENTIAL SOUP COOKBOOK

ESSENTIAL SOUP COOKBOOK

COMFORTING, HEARTY FAVORITES

COMPILED BY JANET ZIMMERMAN

ROCKRIDGE
PRESS

For general information on our other products and services or to obtain technical support, please contact our Customer Care Department within the United States at (866) 744-2665, or outside the United States at (510) 253-0500.

Rockridge Press publishes its books in a variety of electronic and print formats. Some content that appears in print may not be available in electronic books, and vice versa.

TRADEMARKS: Rockridge Press and the Rockridge Press logo are trademarks or registered trademarks of Callisto Media Inc. and/or its affiliates, in the United States and other countries, and may not be used without written permission. All other trademarks are the property of their respective owners. Rockridge Press is not associated with any product or vendor mentioned in this book.

Interior and Cover Designer: Angela Navarra
Art Producer: Meg Baggott
Editor: Anne Lowrey
Production Editor: Ruth Sakata Corley
Production Manager: Riley Hoffman

Cover photo ©2021 Marija Vidal, food styling by Oscar Molinar

Darren Muir, ii, viii, 16, 30, 38, 50, 54, 58, 62, 66, 70, 72, 74, 76, 92, 96; Hélène Dujardin, 14, 64, 78; Linda Xiao, 22; Ivan Solis/ Stocksy Utd, 36; Elysa Weitala, 42; Antonis Achilleos, 46; Evi Abeler, 68; Thomas J. Story, 80, 100; Johnny Autry, 84; AS Food Studio/Shutterstock, 88; Nadine Greeff, 90, 94
Author photo courtesy of Court Mast Photography

ISBN: Print 978-1-63807-301-7
eBook 978-1-63807-178-5
R0

CONTENTS

INTRODUCTION

When I think of the list of my all-time favorite restaurant dishes, I'm surprised at how many of them are soups.
From velvety carrot soup swirled with bright green chive oil at an upscale bistro to savory wonton soup at the neighborhood Chinese take-out place, from an out-of-this-world short rib and caramelized onion soup at my favorite neighborhood restaurant to a rustic tortilla soup from the local Mexican cantina, they're among the best dishes I've ever eaten.

I probably shouldn't be surprised; I think a love of soup was in my genes. As far back as I can remember, my dad loved soup. He always ordered soup on those rare occasions when we went out to dinner and invariably had a bowl of soup for lunch every Saturday. My mother, if not as big a fan as Dad, made soup for dinner often. And why not? With a big family, it was an economical way for her to get a balanced meal on the table. Soup was the perfect way to stretch a sandwich from lunch into a dinner, and that combination was guaranteed to please us kids. So, it was likely predetermined—I was destined to love soup.

When I was learning to cook, soup was a natural place to start. Most soup recipes are straightforward, they rarely require exotic ingredients, and they're wonderfully adaptable. I learned to improvise as a cook by making soups and stews for my college roommates and continued to practice on my friends when I left school. Even today, whenever I don't have the exact ingredients on hand for a given recipe, I can almost always wing it and come up with a pretty good dinner.

Like many cooks, I started out thinking of soup when the weather was cold. My first soups were hearty, warming bowls brimming with chunks of meat and potatoes or noodles. But I soon found recipes that opened my eyes to soups for all seasons—light vegetable soups perfect for the early days of spring and refreshing mixtures that took advantage of fresh summer corn and tomatoes.

That's why I was so excited to work on this book. In it, you'll find 50 recipes for delicious, satisfying soups—classics from across the country and around the world. And if you're new to the world of soup, the opening chapter will give you all the information you need to feel at ease making all kinds of soup varieties, from simple to showstopping. Whether you're cooking for a crowd, a small family, or just yourself, you'll see how soup can fit into any menu.

For me, this book is a wonderful way to spread the word about how soup can change your life. Yeah, maybe I'm kidding about that, but soup has so much going for it—it's healthy, economical, and easy—that I'm sure if you don't already, you'll come to love soup as much as I do.

CHAPTER ONE

SOUP-MAKING ESSENTIALS

I'm not alone in my love of soup. Cooks around the world agree that soup is a fundamental dish in any kitchen, no matter the cuisine or culture. With its constant appearance throughout history, soup has provided sustenance for virtually every person in every region of the world.

Historians date the first soups back some 20,000 years, and they agree that the first restaurants were likely inns where weary travelers could relax and refresh themselves with a sustaining bowl of soup or stew. Plain or fancy, thick and chunky, or brothy and fragrant, it satisfies any appetite. The classic soup recipes in this book will make you a soup expert in no time.

THE ULTIMATE COMFORT FOOD

To me (and I'm sure I'm not the only one), soup is comfort in a bowl. In cuisines around the world, a nourishing crock of soup is the easiest way to welcome dinner guests or feed your family. Who doesn't love a bowl of Matzo Ball Soup (page 44) or Miso Soup (page 77) when suffering from a winter cold? Who would say no to a cup of Creamy Tomato-Basil Soup (page 75) for lunch, with or without a grilled cheese sandwich?

But soup is more than simple comfort food. It fits in with today's sometimes hectic lifestyles—if your family's schedule doesn't allow you to eat at the same time, you can make a batch of soup and keep it warm or reheat it so family members can enjoy it when they come home. It's also economical. Small amounts of meat or fish and the less-than-perfect vegetables from your refrigerator can be stretched into a full meal with the help of broth and flavorings. And soups are a fabulous way to use up leftovers, reducing food waste.

Soup is healthy. Soups almost always include a lot of vegetables, and while people might not agree on what counts as "healthy," pretty much everyone is on board with vegetables. And they will make you a better cook. Soups are a wonderful way to practice all kinds of culinary skills. Chopping all those vegetables will improve your knife work, and soups are a perfect canvas for exploring combinations of ingredients.

Finally, soups are a great way to sample cuisines from across the country and around the globe. Whether it's Minestrone (page 79) from Italy, Beef Pho (page 20) from Vietnam, Russian Borscht (page 71), or regional favorites like New England Clam Chowder (page 99) or Southwestern Turkey Soup (page 52), you'll get a taste of the world without leaving your kitchen.

It's common to think of soup as cold-weather food. Certainly, many soup recipes seem perfect for cool fall nights or stormy winter evenings. But the world of soup is so much more than that. Whether it's a hearty crock of warming White Chicken Chili (page 53) during football season, a bowl of Provençal Pistou Soup (page 82) to welcome spring, or a cooling serving of Gazpacho (page 73) in the summer, soup fits in with any season. And the wonderful variety of soups in this book will appeal to all kinds of appetites, all kinds of diets, and all kinds of cooking skills.

IT'S EASY, TOO!

If you're new to cooking (and even if you're not), you may find the idea of making soup intimidating. For some, soup conjures ideas of making stock from scratch, simmering and skimming vats of meat and vegetables for hours—just to get a base for a dish that will take another day and scores of ingredients to finish. It's easy to see why so many cooks avoid it or buy canned or packaged soups.

But trust me when I say that most soups are easy. Most require a handful of ingredients that you can keep on hand in your pantry or refrigerator. They tend to follow the same general method—sauté, simmer, season—so you'll quickly become proficient at preparing a wide variety of soups from cuisines around the world, especially with the recipes and tips packed into this book. They'll provide all you need to make simple, tasty soups year-round. Many are hearty enough to stand alone as a meal; others require nothing more than a loaf of bread or a quick salad to make a satisfying dinner. Bonus: leftover soup makes the easiest lunch on the planet.

SOUP ESSENTIALS

Chances are, if you've bought this book and read this far, you're eager to start making great soups. But if you're unsure of where to start, I've got you covered. From pantry staples and equipment to tips and tricks on making and storing soup, you'll find everything you need to become a master at soups of all kinds.

THE RIGHT EQUIPMENT

Making great soups doesn't take a whole cupboard of equipment; in fact, you probably have most of what you need already. If not, nothing on this list is very expensive or hard to find, so it's easy to get started.

Soup pot or Dutch oven: This should have a capacity of 4 to 6 quarts and should have a lid. I prefer a shape that's relatively wide in diameter and short in height rather than a tall, narrow pot. Two short handles are better than one long one (unless the pot has an offset handle as well). The material isn't all that important, so long as the bottom is fairly heavy.

Chef's knife: Many soups require a lot of vegetable chopping, so a good-quality, sharp 6- to 8-inch chef's knife will increase your efficiency. If you're purchasing a new knife, consider a Japanese Santoku or Nakiri; both are designed especially for chopping vegetables.

Cutting board: Along with a sharp knife, you'll want a large, sturdy cutting board. Wood or bamboo boards are easy on knives and nice looking as well, but composite (such as Epicurean brand) or plastic boards are fine, too, and can often go in the dishwasher. Lighter-weight boards can be anchored with a damp paper towel or piece of shelf liner if they shift on the counter.

Large, flat bamboo or silicone spoon or spatula: This is not only useful for stirring ingredients but essential for sautéing vegetables. My favorite is a wok spatula, which is rounded on one side and squared off on the other.

Blender: Whether you use a stand blender or immersion (stick) blender is largely a matter of personal preference, but you should have one or both for making pureed soups. I use both. I like a stand blender for velvety smooth soups and use my immersion blender for more rustic soups that are left a bit chunky. If you are buying a new stand blender, look for one that has a large capacity (4 cups with lots of space above) and a vented lid that will allow steam to escape.

Large medium-fine sieve (strainer): This is optional, but if you use a stand blender, passing the pureed soup through a strainer will catch skins and seeds from vegetables, resulting in a silky-smooth mixture. You'll also want a flexible silicone spatula to press the soup through the sieve.

Large liquid measuring cup: A 4-cup glass or plastic measuring cup is handy for measuring stock. Look for one with a sharp pouring spout to decrease dribbling down the side as you pour.

Ladle: Use this for serving. Try to find one with a pouring lip, which will cut down on drips. A capacity of about 1/2 cup is a good size. A hook on the end, instead of a straight handle, will keep the ladle from sliding down into the soup.

Wide, flat soup bowls: These are not essential, but they're my favorite bowl for serving main-dish soups. The wide surface area means more room for garnishes, and I think they look elegant. On the other hand, a few soups work better in smaller, deeper bowls or crocks, such as French Onion Soup (page 59) or soups served as a side dish.

SOUPTACULAR SHORTCUTS

Many of the recipes in this book go together pretty quickly, but let's face it—almost everyone wants to save time on dinner prep, especially during the week. Here are some soup tricks I use when I want to get dinner on the table fast.

USE STORE-BOUGHT STOCK OR BROTH. Believe me, I love using homemade stocks in soup, but honestly, I rarely have them on hand. Commercial stocks and broths have improved so much over the past decade or so that it's not tough to find a good product. My advice is to find a brand you like (low-sodium or salt-free) and stick with it so you always start from the same baseline. You can even keep concentrated broth paste in your refrigerator and add it to water to create a great soup base.

PREHEAT YOUR STOCK. Cold stock can cool down your entire soup pot, increasing the time it takes to come to a simmer. If you're using refrigerated stock or broth, microwave it for a few minutes while you chop or sauté vegetables to speed up the cooking process.

BUY FROZEN VEGETABLES WHEN APPROPRIATE. Of course, you won't always find the right blend, but when it's possible, it'll save a ton of prep time. Just be sure to adjust the cooking time so they don't turn to mush.

BUY FRESH PRE-CHOPPED VEGETABLES. Many produce sections in grocery stores carry chopped onions, carrots, celery, and bell peppers in manageable amounts for soups and stews. They're more expensive than whole vegetables but can be a lifesaver if you're in a hurry. Peeled garlic cloves can also save you time, but avoid pre-chopped garlic, which has to be treated with a chemical that negatively affects the flavor (although frozen minced garlic is a great time-saver).

ESSENTIAL PANTRY ITEMS

Kosher salt: I prefer kosher salt for all my cooking, as it's easy to grab a pinch to season to taste and more difficult to accidentally oversalt. (It's coarser than table salt, so a given volume contains less sodium than fine salt.) If you substitute table or other fine salt in a recipe that calls for kosher salt, use half as much.

Freshly ground black pepper: Freshly ground black pepper is so much more flavorful than pre-ground that it's well worth investing in a pepper grinder.

Spices and dried herbs: Individual ground spices and dried herbs will enliven all your soups. Mixtures like Italian herbs, curry powder, or chili powder can be handy, or you can mix your own from individual products.

Sauces: Sauces like Worcestershire sauce, curry pastes, soy sauce, hoisin, and fish sauce add umami (savory) flavors to soups. Hot sauces like Tabasco, Crystal Hot Sauce, and sriracha are perfect for adding a subtle kick.

Canned goods: Cans of vegetables, such as diced tomatoes and beans, are handy to have for quick soups. Coconut milk is a popular ingredient in some Asian and Caribbean soups. Cans or aseptic packages of stock are essential; low-sodium or salt-free are best so you can season to your own taste and reduce them without ruining the flavor. I like to keep chicken, vegetable, and beef stock in my pantry. There are a couple of good-quality stock concentrates available, such as Better Than Bouillon and More Than Gourmet, but most varieties contain salt, so season accordingly.

Dried goods: Egg noodles and small pasta shapes like farfalle (butterfly shaped) or rotini are best for most American or European soups, while ramen, soba, and udon are more popular in Asian recipes. White and brown rice are also good to have on hand.

Oils: Vegetable and inexpensive olive oils are good for sautéing, while a higher-quality extra-virgin olive oil is great for drizzling over a finished soup.

Wine: Dry white and red wines are used in many of the recipes in this book, with marsala used occasionally. Wine adds acidity and its own flavor, and the alcohol it contains dissolves flavor molecules not soluble in water, so it provides more complex flavors. If you don't drink wine, buy it in four-packs of small bottles so you won't waste the rest of a large bottle. If you can't use wine, try adding a small splash of vinegar and an appropriate amount of stock to replace it. You may also want to add a bit more oil or butter to the recipe because fats dissolve most of the same taste molecules as alcohol.

Refrigerator items: Butter, cream, and Parmesan-style cheese are long-lasting staples that I rely on for delicious soups. (You don't need to splurge on authentic Parmigiano-Reggiano, but look for a good domestic version you can buy whole and in bulk. Pre-grated cheese goes stale quickly. And save the rinds—they're great for adding flavor to broth.) Sturdy vegetables like carrots, celery, and cabbage will last a long time when refrigerated, as will lemons and limes.

Produce: Onions, garlic, and potatoes have a long shelf life if kept in a cool, dark place. Store the potatoes separate from the alliums.

Freezer items: Frozen vegetables can be a time-saver for weeknight soups. You may be able to find minced garlic, ginger, and herbs frozen in cubes; Dorot Gardens is one popular brand.

STORING SOUP

Most soups are great reheated—sometimes they even get better after a day or so. A few simple techniques will ensure that your leftover soups are delicious.

For food safety, it's best to transfer the soup from the pot you cooked it in into a glass or plastic container so it will cool down faster. (Never put hot soup in the refrigerator; cool it first to room temperature.)

Starches such as noodles or rice will continue to absorb liquid as they sit, so you may need to add more stock when reheating. If you're making a big batch of soup and plan to freeze half, don't add starches until after thawing and reheating the second batch.

Freeze soup in portions so you can thaw just want you want for a meal, whether that's lunch for one or a first course for four.

METHODS AND TECHNIQUES

Although soup recipes vary in preparation, there are a handful of techniques you'll see over and over again, which will improve your soup-making and yield delicious, impressive meals.

Sautéing and searing: It might seem like a waste of time to sear meat or to sauté garlic, onions, or other vegetables as a first step, but the higher temperature of the oil for sautéing or searing brings out flavors you can't get at the boiling point of water. It also evaporates some of the water in the vegetables, making their flavor more concentrated, and results in the complex flavors of seared meat.

Deglazing: When searing meat or browning vegetables, you'll end up with browned bits on the bottom of the pan called "fond." Fond has tons of flavor when incorporated into the soup. Chefs call the process of using wine or stock to dissolve the fond "deglazing." You won't always need to do this, but don't skip this step if a recipe calls for it.

Simmering: Some soups require long simmering; tough cuts of meat, dried beans, and sturdy grains need time to soften, generally 1 to 2 hours. But even "quick" soups benefit from simmering for 20 to 30 minutes. Of course, it cooks the ingredients through, giving you tender vegetables and fully cooked meat. But simmering does more than that: as the soup cooks, the flavors blend, which results in a balanced, cohesive soup rather than a mere combination of ingredients.

Layering seasonings: As a soup simmers, ingredients like salt, pepper, spices, and acidic elements will come together, balancing the flavors and seasoning the mixture. Because heat and cooking time can change the effect of these ingredients, I generally add them in stages, using about a third at the beginning and another third after simmering. At that point, taste the soup and see what else it needs—you may not need all the rest, or you may need a bit more.

Balancing flavor: Soups, like sauces, often rely on a balance of tastes: salty, sour, and savory mostly, but sometimes with hints of sweetness or bitterness. Before serving, always taste your soup so you can add any flavor elements that are lacking. (If you're not used to doing this, it's best to ladle some soup out into a cup so you're experimenting with just a little.) If your soup seems one-dimensional and flat, it probably needs either salt or acid or both. Ingredients high in umami— fermented sauces, mushrooms, and aged cheeses—will add a savory, more complex "meaty" flavor.

Pureeing: I often puree vegetable soups, resulting in a more intense flavor and a texture that's thick and creamy. For a rustic texture with a few vegetable chunks, I use an immersion blender. When I want a silky-smooth texture, I use a stand blender. Some soups are delicious regardless of the texture. For example, I like to serve Potato-Leek Soup (page 56) rustic and chunky, but it's equally tasty when smooth and creamy. Do be careful with a stand blender because hot soup will build up steam and can force the top off, which is messy and can be painful. Don't fill the blender jar more than two-thirds full, and hold the lid in place with a dish towel.

Garnishing: Not every recipe in this book includes a garnish, but most soups are enhanced by a drizzle of olive oil, a swirl of cream, or a sprinkling of herbs or cheese. Garnishes provide the finishing touch, improving not only the flavor but also the look of the final dish.

TROUBLESHOOTING

Truth be told, it's kind of difficult to ruin soup, even for beginner cooks. But there are a few common problems that can occur. Fortunately, they're fairly easy to fix.

Soup's too thin?

If you're making a brothy soup, the easiest way to thicken it is to let the liquid reduce, but that only works if the base liquid is under-seasoned. (Otherwise, reducing may make the soup too salty or spicy.) If reducing is not an option, try a cornstarch or flour slurry. Mix 2 tablespoons of cornstarch or flour thoroughly with 2 tablespoons of cold water or stock; then stir it in a teaspoon or so at a time, letting the soup simmer for a minute so the starch can thicken.

Too salty?

If your soup is slightly oversalted, try adding a splash of lemon juice or vinegar, which will help balance out the salt. If the soup is way too salty, the only reliable way to save it is to ladle out about half of the liquid and replace it with unsalted stock. Taste and add a little of the oversalted liquid a few tablespoons at a time until the soup is balanced to your taste.

Too spicy?

As with salt, the best way to reduce the spice level is to remove some of the liquid and replace it with unseasoned stock. Milk or cream can also mitigate the heat of some spices.

Oh no! It's burned?

If only a few of the vegetables on the bottom of the pan are a bit scorched, try to fish out the worst offenders. If the whole bottom layer is burned, taste the soup to see if it tastes burned. If not, ladle the soup off the burned layer into a clean pot, disturbing the soup as little as possible.

ABOUT THE RECIPES

The recipes in this book were chosen with busy cooks in mind. Whenever possible, I've selected streamlined, relatively simple versions of classic soups, which make dinners and lunches a breeze. Most of them contain common, easy-to-find ingredients, and many use only one pot to make cleanup easy as well.

I've included recipes with a wide variety of ingredients and from cuisines around the world so you can find soups to match your tastes and cooking style. Many feature particularly healthy ingredients, while others are more indulgent, like French Onion Soup topped with gooey cheese (page 59). Some, like Hot and Sour Soup (page 69) and Beef Pho (page 20), may introduce you to new ingredients and flavor combinations. Or, when you're in the mood for simple comfort food, soups like Creamy Tomato-Basil Soup (page 75) and Classic Chicken Noodle Soup (page 49) could be just the ticket.

The recipes are divided into chapters based on the main ingredients—meat, poultry, seafood, and vegetables. Keep in mind that most but not all recipes in the Vegetable Soups chapter are strictly vegetarian; they all feature vegetables as the main ingredients, but a few contain meat or meat-based broth.

At the beginning of each recipe, I've included prep and cook times so you can always find a choice that fits your schedule. While I try to be as accurate as possible, keep in mind that several factors, such as your stove, the cooking pot you use, and the temperature of your ingredients, can influence your actual cook time.

You'll also find a "headnote," a short introduction that often explains the history of the recipe or unusual ingredients or preparation methods. I recommend reading the headnote, as it will often contain information designed to ensure the success of the recipe.

Make sure to read all the way through the recipe before you start to cook so you can have your ingredients ready when necessary and know what steps are coming up. This not only makes cooking easier and more pleasurable but also helps ensure that the recipes turn out the way they're supposed to.

LABELS

The recipes are flagged with labels so you can tell at a glance which will meet your particular needs:

Dairy-Free: Contain no milk, cream, or butter or can be made with nondairy milk

45 Minutes or Less: These recipes will be on the table in 45 minutes or less from start to finish, which is very helpful for busy weeknights.

Vegan: Contain no animal products

Vegetarian: Contain no meat or meat products; may contain dairy or eggs

Slow Cooker: These recipes are ideally made low and slow and preferably in a slow cooker. There are stove top tips for each in case you prefer to make it there.

TIPS

Most of the recipes are followed by tips, which make the recipes even more user-friendly. They include:

→ Shortcuts for prep, cooking, and cleanup

→ Make-ahead directions

→ Alternates for unusual ingredients

→ Variations that use different spice profiles or ingredients or accommodate food allergies or dietary preferences

→ Extra information about ingredients, including nutrition facts, or how to select or prep

→ Optional garnishes

→ Storage hints, including how long the soup will keep refrigerated or frozen

Some cooks follow recipes to the letter. Others prefer to improvise, using a recipe as a guide. If you are the second type, soups are generally great candidates for variations. I'd like to offer a few words of advice to those of you who like to wing it in the kitchen: keep track of what you do, either writing in the margins of the recipe (I promise I won't tell your mother), using sticky notes, or even keeping a separate kitchen notebook for your changes. That way, if you come up with a dish your family loves, you'll remember what you did. If your results are not so wonderful, you'll know what to avoid in the future. You'll soon have your own personal collection of favorites.

I hope you enjoy these recipes and come to love making soup as much as I do. Now, let's get cooking!

Beef Pho
(page 20)

MEATY SOUPS AND STEWS

SERVES 6 to 8

45 MINUTES OR LESS

PORK POZOLE VERDE

PREP TIME: **15 minutes**   COOK TIME: **45 minutes**

Pozole is a traditional Mexican soup that features hominy. There are other variations that use a red sauce or white sauce, but this green version includes tomatillos, fresh herbs, heart-healthy avocado, and two types of peppers. You can also top with sliced radishes, shredded cabbage, and minced onions.

2 tablespoons olive oil

1 pound pork
   tenderloin, cubed

Salt

Freshly ground
   black pepper

1 pound tomatillos,
   husked and rinsed

1 large yellow onion,
   coarsely chopped or
   quartered

3 garlic cloves, peeled

2 poblano peppers,
   seeded and chopped

1 serrano pepper, seeded
   and chopped

1 small bunch cilantro,
   chopped (about ¾ cup)

¼ cup loosely packed
   fresh oregano leaves

8 cups low-sodium
   chicken stock

2 (15-ounce) cans white
   hominy, drained
   and rinsed

1 cup shredded Monterey
   Jack cheese, for garnish

1 avocado, diced,
   for garnish

1 lime, cut into wedges,
   for garnish

1. In a large nonstick or cast-iron skillet, heat the olive oil over medium-high heat. Season the pork with salt and pepper; then add the pork to the skillet and sear on all sides, about 5 minutes. Transfer to a plate or bowl to keep warm.

2. Put the tomatillos, onion, garlic, poblano and serrano peppers, cilantro, and oregano in a high-speed blender. Blend until smooth. Pour the mixture into the heated skillet and cook, stirring occasionally, until the color darkens. Remove from the heat.

3. In a large stockpot, bring the stock to a low simmer. Transfer the tomatillo sauce to the stockpot and simmer for 15 minutes, partially covered. Add the seared pork and then the hominy. Stir to combine and return to a simmer. Adjust the seasoning if needed.

4. To serve, ladle into bowls and top with the cheese, avocado, and lime wedges.

CLASSIC BEEF STEW

PREP TIME: 10 minutes   **COOK TIME:** 2 to 3 hours

The delicious aroma of this slow-cooked beef and vegetable stew will fill your home as it slowly simmers in the oven. This is a perfect soup to make ahead, as it tastes even better the next day. Make it over the weekend or when you have time to linger and enjoy the atmosphere the soup creates while it cooks.

2 tablespoons bacon fat

2½ pounds sirloin
   tip roast, cut into
   2-inch cubes

Salt

Freshly ground
   black pepper

1 cup fruity red wine, such
   as zinfandel

1 cup low-sodium
   beef stock

2 tablespoons
   tomato paste

4 white potatoes, cubed

4 carrots, cut into
   2-inch pieces

1 yellow onion, cut
   into eighths

1 rosemary sprig

1. Preheat the oven to 325°F.

2. In a large Dutch oven, melt the bacon fat over medium-high heat. Pat the meat dry with paper towels and season generously with salt and pepper. Sear on all sides. You will likely need to do this in batches to avoid overcrowding the pot. Transfer the browned meat to a separate dish.

3. Deglaze the pan with the red wine, scraping up the browned bits with a wooden spoon and allowing some of the alcohol to evaporate. Whisk in the stock and tomato paste. Return the meat to the pan and add the potatoes, carrots, onion, and rosemary. Give everything a good toss and season generously with salt and pepper.

4. Cover the pot, transfer it to the oven, and cook for 2 to 3 hours or until the meat is fork-tender.

STORAGE TIP: Cool, cover, and store leftovers in the refrigerator for up to 3 days.

VARIATION: To make this soup in a slow cooker, simply place all of the ingredients in a 4-quart slow cooker and cook on low for 6 hours or on high for 2 hours.

BEEF BARLEY SOUP

PREP TIME: **10 minutes**   COOK TIME: **55 minutes**

This hearty soup uses beef chuck and whole-grain barley for a nourishing and comforting dish. Fresh herbs really add to the flavor, so be sure to use what herbs you have on hand, or use dried herbs in their place. Creating a bouquet garni, typically with herbs tied together and made with cheesecloth, allows the flavors to release into the soup.

1 tablespoon olive oil

1 pound beef chuck, cut into ½-inch pieces

Salt

Freshly ground black pepper

1 onion, diced

2 carrots, diced

2 celery stalks, diced

6 garlic cloves, smashed

8 cups low-sodium beef stock

2 tablespoons tomato paste

1½ cups pearl barley

Bouquet garni of fresh herbs, such as rosemary, thyme, and parsley

1. In a large pot, heat the olive oil over medium-high heat. Pat the beef dry with paper towels and season with salt and pepper. Brown on all sides, about 10 minutes total.

2. Add the onion, carrots, celery, and garlic to the pan and cook for 5 minutes, until starting to soften.

3. Pour in the beef stock and tomato paste and bring to a simmer.

4. Add the barley and bouquet garni. Season with salt and pepper, cover the pot, and cook for 40 minutes or until the barley is soft.

5. Remove the herbs and discard. Taste the soup and adjust the seasonings as needed.

STORAGE TIP: Cool, cover, and store leftovers in the refrigerator for up to 4 days.

VARIATION: Barley contains the protein gluten. To make this gluten-free, use brown rice, quinoa, or another gluten-free whole grain.

BEEF PHO

PREP TIME: 20 minutes   **COOK TIME:** 8 to 9 hours on low, 4 to 5 hours on high

Traditionally, pho bo is made with beef marrow and knucklebones, which must be boiled first to allow for the impurities to be released. This recipe uses brisket to speed up the prep time. If you're in a rush, you can throw everything in the slow cooker, but taking the extra few minutes to toast the spices and roast the onions and ginger will release more of the aromatics into your broth.

1 medium yellow onion, quartered

2-inch piece fresh ginger, peeled and halved lengthwise

3 green cardamom pods

1 cinnamon stick

3 whole star anise

1 to 1½ pounds beef brisket

6 cups low-sodium beef stock

3 cups water

3 garlic cloves, smashed

2 tablespoons fish sauce

2 teaspoons sugar

Salt (optional)

14 ounces rice noodles

8 ounces top round steak, very thinly sliced crosswise

Fresh Thai basil, for serving

Fresh cilantro, for serving

Fresh mint leaves, for serving

Mung bean sprouts, for serving

Jalapeños, seeded and thinly sliced, for serving

White onion, thinly sliced, for serving

Lime wedges, for serving

Hoisin sauce, for serving

Sriracha, for serving

1. Preheat the oven to 425°F.

2. On a baking sheet, arrange the onion and ginger and roast until lightly charred, about 10 minutes. Alternatively, you can pan roast them on the stove in a lightly oiled pan over medium-high heat.

3. In a small, dry skillet over medium heat, toast the cardamom pods, cinnamon stick, and star anise for 3 to 4 minutes.

4. In the slow cooker, combine the roasted onion and ginger with the toasted spice mixture. Add the beef brisket, beef stock, water, garlic, fish sauce, and sugar.

5. Cover and cook on low for 8 to 9 hours or on high for 4 to 5 hours.

6. Skim any solids or fat from the surface of the soup. Strain the soup through a fine-mesh sieve into a large stockpot. Place the pot on the stove over medium-low heat to keep warm.

7. Remove the brisket from the sieve and slice it thinly across the grain. Discard everything else from the sieve.

8. Season with additional fish sauce or salt (if using).

9. Cook the rice noodles according to package instructions. Drain; then divide the noodles among bowls.

10. In each bowl, place several slices of brisket and a few slices of the raw top round on top of the noodles. Ladle the broth into each bowl.

11. Serve alongside Thai basil, cilantro, mint, bean sprouts, jalapeños, lime wedges, hoisin sauce, and sriracha.

PREP TIP: To save time, prep the aromatics and spices (steps 1 to 3) the night before, and refrigerate until ready to use.

VARIATION: To cook on the stove top, combine the stock ingredients (step 4) in a large stockpot. Bring to a simmer and cook, covered, for 3 to 4 hours, or until the beef is tender. Spoon or blot off the fat from the surface of the broth. Use a fine-mesh strainer to scoop out the solids. Place the pot back on the stove over low heat. Continue at step 7.

ITALIAN SAUSAGE LASAGNA SOUP

PREP TIME: 15 minutes   COOK TIME: 35 minutes

Lasagna can be a labor of love, but the work is worth it for a beautiful, layered pasta dish packed with flavor. This soup has lasagna's hearty components, but it can be made quickly in only one pot. Serve it with a sprinkle of fresh basil, a dollop of ricotta, and, if you like, some bread on the side.

10 lasagna noodles, each noodle broken into 2 or 3 pieces

1 pound Italian sausage

1 cup diced onion

3 garlic cloves, minced

1 tablespoon Italian seasoning

2 tablespoons tomato paste

3 cups low-sodium chicken stock

1 (28-ounce) can diced tomatoes

⅓ cup grated Parmesan cheese

¼ cup half-and-half

Ricotta cheese, for serving

Fresh basil, for serving

1. Cook the lasagna noodles according to the package directions until al dente. Drain and set aside while preparing the rest of the soup.

2. In a large pot, combine the sausage and onion. Cook over medium heat for 8 to 10 minutes, stirring, until the onion is translucent and the sausage is crumbled and browned. Add the garlic and cook for 1 minute more, until fragrant.

3. Stir in the Italian seasoning, tomato paste, chicken stock, and tomatoes and their juices. Bring to a boil. Reduce the heat to low and simmer the soup for 10 minutes.

4. Stir in the Parmesan cheese and half-and-half. Simmer for 10 minutes more.

5. Add the cooked noodles. Divide the soup among 4 individual bowls and top with a dollop of ricotta and a sprinkling of fresh basil.

STORAGE TIP: This soup will keep, refrigerated in an airtight container, for 2 to 3 days.

ITALIAN WEDDING SOUP

PREP TIME: 15 minutes   COOK TIME: 30 minutes

Often when a dish is adopted by a new culture, it takes on a completely original flavor not present in the original dish. Italian wedding soup is a classic example. Wedding soup, as we know it, is largely an American creation, a mistranslation of the Italian *minestra maritata*, which refers to the delicious marriage of meat and vegetables. So, while you won't find this version on the menu in Italy, it is filling and delicious, and it's just a lovely sounding name.

½ cup bread crumbs

¼ cup milk

½ pound ground veal

¾ pound ground pork

1 teaspoon minced garlic

1 teaspoon dried oregano

1 large egg, lightly beaten

⅔ cup finely grated
    Parmesan cheese

Salt

Freshly ground
    black pepper

2 tablespoons olive oil

1 onion, diced

2 carrots, diced

2 celery stalks, diced

½ cup dry white wine

8 cups low-sodium
    chicken stock

4 ounces orzo pasta

1 bunch Lacinato kale,
    ribs removed, leaves
    thinly sliced

4 cups thinly sliced
    spinach leaves

1 cup coarsely chopped
    fresh basil leaves

1. Preheat the oven to 375°F. Line a baking sheet with parchment paper.

2. In a small bowl, soak the bread crumbs in the milk; set aside.

3. In a large mixing bowl, mix the veal, pork, garlic, oregano, egg, and Parmesan. Squeeze the excess milk out of the bread crumbs and add the bread crumbs to the meat mixture. Season with salt and pepper. Mix with your hands.

4. Form the meat mixture into about 36 teaspoon-size meatballs and place them on the prepared baking sheet. Bake for 25 minutes, until browned.

5. While the meatballs bake, in a large pot over medium heat, heat the olive oil and add the onion, carrots, celery, and a generous pinch of salt. Cook for 10 minutes, stirring frequently, until the vegetables have softened.

6. Add the white wine and sauté for 2 to 3 minutes to cook off some of the alcohol. Pour in the chicken stock and bring to a simmer.

7. Add the pasta and cook for 5 minutes, until soft.

8. Add the kale and the meatballs and cook for 2 minutes. Remove the pot from the heat and stir in the spinach and basil. Season with salt and pepper.

9. Serve immediately or chill, cover, and store leftovers in the refrigerator for up to 4 days.

VARIATION: To make this soup free of wheat and gluten, use gluten-free bread crumbs and gluten-free pasta.

PORK AND NAVY BEAN STEW

PREP TIME: 10 minutes   **COOK TIME:** 1 hour 15 minutes

Pork and beans served as the inspiration for this savory stew, but this version is more of a meal than a side dish. You can use any variety of canned beans you enjoy in this soup; just make sure to drain and rinse them before adding to the soup.

2 tablespoons olive oil

1 yellow onion, diced

2 celery stalks, coarsely chopped

2 carrots, coarsely chopped

2 pounds boneless pork roast, cut into 1-inch pieces

Salt

Freshly ground black pepper

8 cups low-sodium chicken stock

2 chipotles in adobo sauce, plus 1 tablespoon adobo sauce

¼ cup tomato paste

1 tablespoon packed brown sugar

2 (15-ounce) cans navy beans, drained and rinsed

1 teaspoon apple cider vinegar

8 ounces sour cream, for serving

1 cup fresh cilantro leaves, for serving

1. In a large pot, heat the olive oil and cook the onion, celery, and carrots for 5 minutes, until slightly softened.

2. Push the vegetables to the sides of the pot. Season the meat with salt and pepper and brown on all sides in the center of the pot, about 10 minutes total.

3. Pour in the chicken stock and add the chipotles, adobo, tomato paste, and brown sugar. Cover and cook for 1 hour, or until the pork is tender. Add the navy beans and vinegar and cook until just heated through. Adjust seasoning to taste.

4. Serve with the sour cream and cilantro.

5. Cool, cover, and store leftovers in the refrigerator for up to 4 days.

INGREDIENT TIP: Always read the labels on canned goods to check for the presence of allergens. Some varieties of chipotles contain soybean oil and/or wheat.

SERVES 4 to 6

DAIRY-FREE

CLASSIC BEEF CHILI

PREP TIME: **15 minutes**   COOK TIME: **45 minutes**

This beef chili opts for ground beef to speed up the cooking process and create a delicious hearty chili in under an hour. The flavor of the meat permeates the stew, so it's worth it to purchase good-quality grass-fed beef if you're able to.

1½ pounds ground beef

Salt

Freshly ground black pepper

2 yellow onions, diced

4 carrots, diced

2 celery stalks, diced

2 red bell peppers, cored and thinly sliced

2 (15-ounce) cans diced fire-roasted tomatoes

1 (15-ounce) can kidney beans, drained and rinsed

1 tablespoon ancho chili powder

1 tablespoon smoked paprika

1 tablespoon ground cumin

1 teaspoon ground cinnamon

¼ teaspoon curry powder (optional)

¼ teaspoon ground cayenne pepper

1. Heat a large pot over medium-high heat. Season the meat with salt and pepper. In the heated pot, brown the meat for 5 to 10 minutes, stirring occasionally.

2. Add the onions, carrots, celery, and bell peppers and cook for another 5 minutes, until slightly softened.

3. Stir in the tomatoes, beans, chili powder, paprika, cumin, cinnamon, curry powder (if using), and cayenne pepper and cook for 30 minutes, to allow the vegetables to soften further and all of the flavors to come together.

4. To serve, ladle the chili into individual serving bowls. Cool, cover, and store leftovers in the refrigerator for up to 4 days.

BEEF BOURGUIGNON

PREP TIME: 10 minutes, plus 6 hours to marinate   **COOK TIME:** 3 hours

This rich French beef stew was made famous in America by Julia Child. It undoubtedly started its life as a humble peasant dish used to cook tougher pieces of beef. It is prepared with beef simmered in the red wine it marinates in overnight, along with pearl onions, bacon, and mushrooms.

2 pounds beef chuck, cut into 2-inch pieces (see tip)

1 (750-ml) bottle red burgundy or other pinot noir

1 bay leaf

1 thyme sprig

1 tablespoon rendered pork lard, duck fat, or unsalted butter

4 ounces slab bacon, cubed

16 pearl onions, peeled (see tip)

8 ounces small button mushrooms, trimmed

Salt

Cracked black peppercorns

2 celery stalks, finely diced

2 carrots, diced

1 tablespoon flour

6 cups low-sodium beef stock

⅓ cup coarsely chopped parsley, for garnish

1. In a large nonreactive bowl, combine the beef, wine, bay leaf, and thyme. Cover, and marinate in the refrigerator for a minimum of 6 hours, preferably overnight.

2. In a large Dutch oven or stockpot, heat the lard over medium heat. Add the bacon and cook until lightly browned, stirring, about 5 minutes. Add the onions and cook, stirring occasionally, until lightly browned, about 10 minutes. With a slotted spoon, transfer the onions and bacon to a plate. Add the mushrooms to the pot and cook, stirring occasionally, until lightly browned, about 3 minutes. Transfer to the plate with the onions and bacon.

3. With tongs, remove the beef from the marinade, reserving the marinade. Pat the beef dry with paper towels. Season with salt and cracked peppercorns. Turn the heat to medium-high. Working in batches, brown the beef on all sides, about 10 minutes per batch. Transfer the beef to a plate.

4. Add the celery and carrots to the pot and cook until soft and lightly browned, stirring occasionally, about 5 minutes. Sprinkle the flour over top and stir in the vegetables. Add the reserved marinade, stock, and beef, and bring to a boil over high heat. Reduce the heat to a simmer, cover, and cook for 2 hours. The meat should remain partially submerged in liquid; if it starts to look a little dry, add more water, red wine, or stock.

5. If you want a more refined dish, transfer the beef to a plate; place a fine-mesh strainer over a large bowl and strain the sauce, discarding the carrots, celery, and garlic. Return the beef to the pot. Add the mushrooms, bacon, and onions. Simmer until the beef is fork-tender, about 1 hour.

6. Sprinkle with the parsley and serve.

INGREDIENT TIP: An easy way to peel pearl onions is to trim off the root end, drop them into boiling water for 30 seconds, drain, transfer to a bowl of ice water, and drain again. You should then be able to squeeze them right out of their peels. You can also buy these frozen.

INGREDIENT TIP: What cut of beef is best to use? I generally use meat from the shoulder (like chuck), oxtail, short ribs, or shanks. Traditionally, a calf's foot is included; the considerable collagen it contains makes for a deliciously rich and unctuous result. You can find them in Asian or Mexican markets.

GARLIC-ROSEMARY BRAISED LAMB AND BEANS

PREP TIME: 10 minutes, plus 15 minutes for resting   **COOK TIME:** 1 hour 40 minutes

This hearty stew includes pungent rosemary and garlic, tender braised lamb, and soft white beans. Browning the meat first is a typical preparation for stews, but braising in liquid is a healthier method for preparing meat and is the process used here.

2 tablespoons olive oil

2 shallots, thinly sliced

1½ pounds lamb shoulder, cut into 2-inch pieces

2 tablespoons minced fresh rosemary leaves

Salt

Freshly ground black pepper

2 cups low-sodium chicken stock

½ cup dry red wine

4 garlic cloves, smashed

1 (15-ounce) can great northern or cannellini beans

1. Preheat the oven to 350°F.

2. In a large Dutch oven, heat the olive oil over medium-high heat. Add the shallots and cook for 2 minutes.

3. Pat the lamb dry with paper towels and generously season it with the rosemary, salt, and pepper. Add it to the pan along with the chicken stock, red wine, and garlic. Bring the mixture to a simmer. Cover the pan and transfer it to the oven. Cook for 1½ hours, or until the lamb is very tender.

4. Stir in the beans. Let the stew rest for 15 minutes before serving.

VARIATION: If you prefer beef, use chuck roast in place of the lamb.

SLOW COOKER SHOYU RAMEN

PREP TIME: 20 minutes, plus 1 hour to marinate
COOK TIME: 7 to 8 hours on low, 3 to 4 hours on high

Ramen is a hearty and magical noodle soup that can be labor-intensive and complicated. This simplified version uses a slow cooker to take out some of the work while also stepping it up a notch from the instant ramen packets you get at the grocery store. Dashi powder can be purchased in an Asian grocery store or online. If you cannot find it, just substitute more chicken stock for the dashi stock. This shoyu-based ramen will satisfy your ramen craving at home.

FOR THE MARINADE

½ cup soy sauce

¼ cup mirin

¼ cup sake

1 tablespoon brown sugar

3 garlic cloves, smashed

2-inch piece fresh ginger, peeled and grated

1 tablespoon vegetable oil

½ teaspoon freshly ground black pepper

1½ to 2 pounds pork shoulder

FOR THE SOUP

1 teaspoon vegetable oil

4 cups low-sodium chicken stock

4 cups dashi stock (2 teaspoons dashi powder dissolved in 4 cups hot water)

1 medium yellow onion, quartered

3 garlic cloves, smashed

2-inch piece fresh ginger, peeled and sliced

5 tablespoons soy sauce

1 tablespoon mirin

1 tablespoon sake

1 teaspoon sesame oil

1 pound uncooked ramen

OPTIONAL TOPPINGS

Scallions, both white and green parts, finely chopped

Corn kernels

Soft-boiled eggs, halved

Mung bean sprouts, blanched

Nori

Shichimi (Japanese seven-spice blend)

TO MAKE THE MARINADE

1. In a large bowl or resealable bag, combine the soy sauce, mirin, sake, brown sugar, garlic, ginger, oil, and pepper. Add the pork and turn to coat. Cover and marinate in the refrigerator for 1 hour or as long as overnight.

2. In a large pan, heat the vegetable oil over medium-high heat. Take the pork out of the marinade and brown it on all sides in the pan, 3 to 5 minutes. Discard the marinade.

3. Transfer the pork to the slow cooker; then add the chicken stock, dashi stock, onion, garlic, and ginger.

4. Cover and cook on low for 7 to 8 hours or on high for 3 to 4 hours.

5. Remove the pork, ginger, garlic, and onion from the slow cooker. Skim off any fats or solids with a sieve until the stock is clear. You can also strain the stock through a sieve into a large heatproof bowl and then pour it back into the slow cooker.

6. Add the soy sauce, mirin, sake, and sesame oil to the slow cooker.

7. Cover and cook on high for 15 minutes.

8. Meanwhile, cut the pork into thin slices.

9. In a large pot, cook the ramen according to the package instructions. Drain the noodles and divide among bowls.

10. Ladle the stock over the noodles and top with a few slices of pork. Add scallions, corn, one or two soft-boiled egg halves, mung bean sprouts, nori, and shichimi, as desired, and serve.

PREP TIP: Prepare as many toppings as you like beforehand so that you can quickly assemble the ramen when serving. For an even simpler preparation, just season the pork with salt and refrigerate it at least 1 hour or as long as overnight instead of marinating the meat.

VARIATION: To cook on the stove top, use a large pot to brown the pork in step 1. Pour off any fat; then add the stock ingredients to the pot. Bring to a simmer; then cover and cook for 1¼ to 2 hours. At step 7, bring to a simmer over medium heat and cook for 10 minutes.

HOMESTYLE BEEF AND VEGETABLE SOUP

PREP TIME: 10 minutes   **COOK TIME:** 1 hour 5 minutes

Whether you're a meat-and-potatoes person or tend to prefer vegetables, you'll find this soup satisfying. It's great to take to potluck dinners, and it is the perfect choice in chilly weather. Make a pot of this and keep it in your freezer—you'll thank me later.

1 tablespoon olive oil

1 pound top round beef, cubed

1 small yellow onion, chopped

4 cups low-sodium beef stock

1 (14-ounce) can diced fire-roasted tomatoes

1 pound frozen mixed vegetables

2 medium potatoes, peeled and cut into 1-inch cubes

Salt

Freshly ground black pepper

1. In a Dutch oven, heat the olive oil over medium heat. Add the beef and sauté until it starts to brown. Add the onion and cook for 5 to 7 minutes, until translucent.

2. Add the stock and tomatoes and their juices. Cover and simmer on low for about 40 minutes or until the meat is fork-tender.

3. Add the soup vegetables and potatoes. Cook for 15 more minutes, or until the potatoes and vegetables are tender, stirring occasionally. You can add a little water while cooking if the soup gets too thick.

4. Season with salt and pepper, and serve.

VARIATION: You can swap out the potatoes for ½ cup of dried orzo or another small pasta (gluten-free if needed). Keep an eye on the cooking time, though, as the orzo will cook faster than the potatoes.

SWEDISH MEATBALL SOUP WITH CABBAGE AND PASTA

PREP TIME: 15 minutes   **COOK TIME:** 35 minutes

In the darkest days of winter, the warm spices in the meatballs and the sturdy beef stock offer warmth and comfort. To save time, you can use premade Swedish meatballs (without gravy) if you wish.

1 white bread slice, crusts removed

¼ cup milk

8 ounces ground beef

8 ounces ground pork

¼ cup minced onion

¼ teaspoon ground allspice

¼ teaspoon freshly ground nutmeg

1 large egg, lightly beaten

Salt

Freshly ground black pepper

8 cups low-sodium beef stock

8 ounces elbow macaroni noodles

4 cups coarsely chopped cabbage leaves

1. Preheat the oven to 375°F. Line a baking sheet with parchment paper.

2. In a medium bowl, soak the bread in the milk. Set aside.

3. In a mixing bowl, mix the beef, pork, onion, allspice, and nutmeg. Wring the excess milk from the bread and add the bread to the meat mixture. Pour the egg over the mixture. Season with salt and pepper and mix well with your hands.

4. Form the meat mixture into about 24 medium-size meatballs and place them on the prepared baking sheet. Bake for 30 minutes until browned.

5. During the last 10 minutes of baking time, bring the beef stock to a simmer in a large pot and cook the macaroni noodles for 5 minutes.

6. Add the cabbage and meatballs to the stock and cook for 5 minutes. Season with salt and pepper. Serve immediately.

STORAGE TIP: Cool, cover, and store leftovers in the refrigerator for up to 4 days.

Matzo Ball Soup
(page 44)

CHAPTER THREE

POULTRY SOUPS AND STEWS

THAI COCONUT CURRY SOUP WITH CHICKEN

PREP TIME: 15 minutes   **COOK TIME:** 15 minutes

Red curry is always a favorite dish at Thai restaurants, and this soup version delivers on the same notable flavors. The red curry paste infuses the coconut milk with a rich spiciness that is just right. This recipe includes the traditional Thai vegetables—green beans, mushrooms, and tomatoes—but you can use whatever vegetables you have on hand.

1 tablespoon coconut oil or olive oil

1 yellow onion, halved and thinly sliced

2 garlic cloves, minced

2 tablespoons red curry paste

1 tablespoon coconut sugar or light brown sugar

1 tablespoon fish sauce

1 (14-ounce) can full-fat coconut milk

8 cups low-sodium chicken stock

4 ounces thin green beans, trimmed and cut into 2-inch pieces

4 ounces cremini mushrooms, halved

2 plum tomatoes, quartered

2 tablespoons freshly squeezed lime juice

2 cups shredded cooked chicken

Handful fresh cilantro, coarsely chopped, for garnish

1. In a large pot, heat the coconut oil over medium-high heat. Add the onion and sauté for 5 minutes, until gently browned on the edges.

2. Stir in the garlic, curry paste, and coconut sugar. Cook for about 1 minute, until fragrant. Add the fish sauce, coconut milk, and chicken stock. Bring the soup to a simmer.

3. Add the green beans and mushrooms and cook for 2 minutes.

4. Add the tomatoes and cook for 1 minute more. Stir in the lime juice and chicken, simmering the soup for 3 to 4 minutes, until the chicken is just warmed through.

5. Divide the soup among serving dishes and top with the cilantro.

GINGER CHICKEN ZOODLE SOUP

PREP TIME: 20 minutes   COOK TIME: 15 minutes

For a lighter and refreshing take on classic chicken noodle soup, use fresh ginger and tender zucchini noodles. Replacing the traditional pasta with vegetables makes the soup naturally gluten-free. Zucchini noodles, or zoodles, are a healthy and light alternative to spaghetti.

2 zucchini	2 garlic cloves, minced	4 cups shredded
Salt	1 carrot, sliced	cooked chicken
1 tablespoon canola oil	1 celery stalk, minced	
1 tablespoon minced	8 cups low-sodium	
peeled fresh ginger	chicken stock	

1. Trim the stem ends from the zucchini and halve them widthwise so you have 2 segments, each about 4 inches long. One at a time, fit them onto a spiralizer and run them through the smallest noodle setting. Spread the noodles out in a colander and generously season with salt. Place the colander in the sink and let it sit for 10 minutes.

2. Meanwhile, in a large pot over medium heat, heat the canola oil. Add the ginger, garlic, carrot, celery, and a pinch of salt. Cook for 5 minutes until the vegetables begin to soften, being careful not to burn the garlic.

3. Add the chicken stock and bring the soup to a simmer. Cook for 5 minutes.

4. Rinse the zucchini noodles under cool running water and squeeze excess moisture from the noodles with your hands. Add the noodles and chicken to the pot. Simmer for 2 to 3 minutes, until just heated through. Serve immediately, or cover and refrigerate for up to 2 days.

PREP TIP: Leaving the zucchini peel on retains more nutrients, but if you prefer an appearance more like traditional pasta, peel the zucchini before running it through the spiralizer.

CUBAN-STYLE CHICKEN STEW

PREP TIME: 10 minutes, plus 1 hour to marinate   **COOK TIME:** 45 minutes

This stew includes several classic Cuban ingredients, which are easy to find in any grocery store. Bone-in chicken thighs infuse rich flavor in the broth, and the chicken is fall-off-the-bone delicious by the time the soup is ready.

5 tablespoons olive oil, divided

Zest and juice of 1 lime

Zest and juice of 1 orange

4 garlic cloves, minced

1 teaspoon ground cumin

1 teaspoon dried oregano

2 pounds bone-in, skin-on chicken thighs

Salt

Freshly ground black pepper

1 green bell pepper, thinly sliced

1 onion, halved and thinly sliced

½ cup dry white wine

4 cups peeled and diced white potatoes

2 cups low-sodium chicken stock

1 cup frozen peas

2 tablespoons tomato paste

⅓ cup pepper-stuffed olives

¼ cup raisins

2 tablespoons capers

2 tablespoons fresh flat-leaf parsley, for garnish

1. In a large bowl, mix 4 tablespoons of olive oil with the lime and orange zest and juices and the garlic, cumin, and oregano. Coat the chicken thighs in this mixture and place in the refrigerator to marinate for at least 1 hour.

2. Remove the chicken from the marinade and pat dry. Season generously with salt and pepper.

3. In a large pot, heat the remaining 1 tablespoon of olive oil over medium heat. Sear the chicken on both sides in the oil. Transfer to a separate plate to rest.

4. In the pot, cook the pepper and onion for 5 minutes, until slightly softened. Deglaze the pan with the white wine and add the potatoes, chicken stock, peas, and tomato paste. Return the chicken to the pot, cover, and cook for 30 minutes, until the chicken is cooked through and the potatoes are soft.

5. Add the olives, raisins, and capers and cook for another 5 minutes. Adjust the seasonings as necessary. Garnish with the parsley.

CHICKEN TORTILLA SOUP WITH LIME AND AVOCADO

PREP TIME: 15 minutes   **COOK TIME:** 8 to 10 hours

This delightful soup is tangy, filling, and packed with flavors you'll love. The creamy avocado, black beans, tangy tomatoes, and chicken taste perfect together. A hearty dose of cilantro is the ideal fresh garnish. Most of all, though, it couldn't be easier to make—simply place the ingredients into the pot and come home to a piping-hot soup almost ready to serve.

1 pound boneless, skinless chicken breast, trimmed

4 cups low-sodium chicken stock

1 (15-ounce) can black beans, drained and rinsed

1 (14.5-ounce) can diced tomatoes, drained

1 (10-ounce) can diced tomatoes with green chilies, drained

1 yellow onion, diced

3 garlic cloves, minced

2 limes, divided

1 cup coarsely chopped fresh cilantro

1 avocado, peeled, halved, pitted, and diced

2 (6-inch) corn tortillas, cut into strips

1. In a slow cooker, combine the chicken, chicken stock, black beans, diced tomatoes, tomatoes with green chilies, onion, and garlic. Cover the cooker and cook on low heat for 8 to 10 hours, until the chicken is cooked through.

2. Using two forks, shred the chicken.

3. Juice 1½ of the limes and add the juice to the slow cooker, reserving the remaining lime half. Stir in the cilantro, avocado, and tortilla strips.

4. Cut the remaining lime half into 4 wedges. Serve the soup with a lime wedge.

VARIATION: To prepare this soup on the stove top, in a large pot or Dutch oven over medium heat, heat 1 tablespoon of olive oil. Add the onion and garlic and cook, stirring occasionally, for 10 to 12 minutes, or until the onion begins to brown. Add the chicken stock, diced tomatoes, tomatoes with green chilies, black beans, and chicken to the pot and bring to a boil. Reduce the heat to medium-low, cover the pot, and cook for about 25 minutes, or until the chicken can be easily shredded with two forks. Finish the recipe as instructed in steps 3 and 4.

MATZO BALL SOUP

PREP TIME: 30 minutes, plus 30 minutes to chill   **COOK TIME:** 1 hour 20 minutes

Matzo ball soup is often made with chicken stock, but this version uses an easy homemade vegetable broth that simmers while you make the matzo balls. This comforting soup is easy to make and perfect for when you are feeling a little under the weather.

FOR THE SOUP

2 tablespoons olive oil

2 medium
   onions, chopped

6 medium carrots, cut
   into coins (about
   1 pound)

4 celery stalks, trimmed
   and chopped (about
   ½ pound)

1 parsnip, peeled and
   cut into coins

6 garlic cloves, smashed

1½ teaspoons fresh
   grated ginger

10 ounces cremini
   mushrooms, trimmed
   and chopped

1 medium zucchini, halved
   lengthwise and cut into
   half-moons

8 cups water

3 tablespoons fresh
   chopped basil, or
   1 tablespoon frozen or
   dried basil

2 teaspoons kosher salt

FOR THE MATZO BALLS

2 tablespoons vegeta-
   ble stock

4 large eggs

1 cup matzo meal

¼ cup olive oil

2 tablespoons finely
   chopped fresh
   dill fronds

1 teaspoon kosher salt

½ teaspoon
   ground ginger

TO MAKE THE SOUP

1. In a large stockpot, heat the olive oil over medium-high heat. Add the onions, carrots, celery, and parsnip. Cook, stirring frequently so the vegetables don't brown,
   until the onions are soft and translucent, about 10 minutes.

2. Add the garlic and ginger. Sauté for 1 minute, or until fragrant. Add the mushrooms
   and cook, stirring frequently, until they release their juices, 5 to 7 minutes. When
   most of the mushroom liquid has cooked off, add the zucchini and sauté until it
   begins to soften, 3 to 5 minutes.

3. Add the water. Turn the heat to high and bring to a boil. Stir in the basil and salt.
   Lower the heat and simmer, partially covered, for 45 to 60 minutes.

4. While the soup is simmering, transfer a couple of tablespoons of the simmering stock from the stockpot to a small bowl to cool slightly. In a large bowl, beat the eggs. Mix in the matzo meal, olive oil, cooled vegetable stock, dill, salt, and ginger. Stir with a fork until well mixed. Cover and chill in the refrigerator for 30 minutes.

5. In the meantime, bring a large pot of salted water to a boil. When you are ready to make the matzo balls, scoop up a walnut-size piece of the chilled mixture with oiled hands and roll it into a ball between your palms, taking care not to compress it. Drop it in the water, and continue forming matzo balls, being careful not to crowd the pot. You may need to cook the matzo balls in batches.

6. Gently stir to dislodge any matzo balls that may have stuck to the bottom. Return to a boil, lower the heat, and simmer, covered, for 25 to 30 minutes, until the matzo balls have lightened in color, are cooked through, and have about doubled in size.

7. While the matzo balls are cooking, strain the broth. Set a large colander over another soup pot. Carefully pour the soup from the stockpot through the colander. Set aside some of the carrot and parsnip slices; then gently press on the vegetables in the colander with a spoon to extract the broth. If you don't have another soup pot, another option is set the colander over a large bowl and transfer the veggies to it with a slotted spoon. Reserve some veggies, and press on the rest with the back of the spoon. Lift out the colander and pour the broth that has collected in the bowl back into the stockpot.

8. Return the reserved carrots and parsnips to the broth. If you'll be serving the soup right away, bring it to a simmer and add the prepared matzo balls. When the soup and matzo balls are hot, ladle into bowls and serve.

PREP TIP: You can make the broth 1 to 2 days in advance and refrigerate, covered, until ready to use. Or divide it among freezer-safe containers and freeze for up to 3 months. You can also prepare the matzo balls a day ahead. When they are cooked through, transfer them to an airtight container using a slotted spoon. Reheat in simmering broth.

LEMON CHICKEN ORZO SOUP

PREP TIME: 15 minutes **COOK TIME:** 50 minutes

Here, a traditional chicken soup is remade with Mediterranean flavors including thyme, oregano, and lemon. Tender chicken is complemented by a vibrant lemony broth and orzo pasta. It's a crowd-pleaser all around.

2 ounces orzo pasta

12 ounces boneless, skinless chicken breast

6 cups low-sodium chicken stock, divided

1 tablespoon olive oil

2 medium carrots, diced

2 celery stalks, diced

½ medium onion, diced

1 garlic clove, minced

½ teaspoon dried thyme

½ teaspoon dried oregano

¼ teaspoon freshly ground black pepper

1 bay leaf

Zest and juice of 1 large lemon

2 cups spinach leaves

1. Bring a large pot of water to a boil. Add the orzo and cook until al dente according to the package directions. Drain.

2. Meanwhile, in a small pot, combine the chicken and 2 cups of chicken stock. Bring to a boil; then quickly reduce the heat to a simmer, partially cover, and cook for 5 to 10 minutes, or until the chicken is no longer pink in the center. Remove from the heat and let stand in the hot chicken stock for 20 minutes.

3. In a stockpot, heat the olive oil over medium-high heat. Add the carrots, celery, and onion and cook for 5 to 7 minutes, or until the vegetables have softened and the onion is translucent. Add the garlic and cook for 1 minute. Season with the thyme, oregano, and pepper. Add the remaining 4 cups of chicken stock and the bay leaf and bring the mixture to a boil. Partially cover, reduce the heat, and simmer for 10 minutes.

4. Add the lemon zest, lemon juice, drained orzo, and spinach to the soup. Shred the chicken and add it to the soup along with the stock used to cook it. Continue to cook for 2 to 3 minutes, or until the spinach is wilted. Remove the bay leaf. Serve hot.

WILD RICE AND TURKEY SOUP

PREP TIME: 10 minutes   **COOK TIME:** 1 hour

This simple soup is perfect for the day after Thanksgiving to use up turkey leftovers. Dark meat works well in this soup, but you can use whatever you have on hand as well. It's an easy recipe designed to give you a break in the kitchen. Feel free to thicken the soup with a few scoops of mashed potatoes as well, if you have extra.

2 tablespoons olive oil

1 onion, diced

4 celery stalks, diced

4 carrots, diced

8 cups low-sodium
  chicken stock

Salt

Freshly ground
  black pepper

1 bay leaf

1 cup wild rice

4 cups shredded
  cooked turkey

1. In a large pot, heat the olive oil over medium heat and cook the onion, celery, and carrots for 10 minutes, until they have softened.

2. Pour in the chicken stock, season generously with salt and pepper, and add the bay leaf.

3. Bring to a simmer and stir in the wild rice.

4. Cover and cook for 45 minutes, or until the rice is al dente. Stir in the turkey and simmer until it's heated through. Remove the bay leaf.

STORAGE TIP: Cool, cover, and store leftovers in the refrigerator for up to 3 days.

VARIATION: If you don't have turkey, feel free to use shredded cooked chicken instead.

CLASSIC CHICKEN NOODLE SOUP

PREP TIME: 10 minutes   **COOK TIME:** 25 minutes

This soul-warming soup instantly evokes comfort and healing. It may bring back memories of being served chicken noodle soup by a loved one when you were feeling sick. You may even swear that you're feeling better immediately after that first sip. The onions, carrots, and celery contain vitamins A and C and other antioxidants that have been known to build a strong immune system. This soup's flavor and nourishment are classic for a reason.

3 tablespoons olive oil

1 large onion, chopped

3 large carrots, chopped

4 celery stalks, chopped

4 garlic cloves, minced

10 cups low-sodium chicken stock

8 ounces egg noodles

4 cups shredded cooked chicken breast

Salt

Freshly ground black pepper

½ cup chopped fresh parsley leaves

1. In a large stockpot, heat the olive oil over medium-high heat. Add the onion, carrots, and celery, stirring frequently until the vegetables are tender, about 15 minutes.

2. Add the garlic and cook for an additional 1 minute or until fragrant. Add the stock and bring to a boil.

3. Add the egg noodles and cook for 6 minutes. Then add the shredded chicken and cook for an additional 2 minutes, until the noodles are cooked through and the chicken has warmed.

4. Season with salt and pepper to taste. Stir in the parsley.

INGREDIENT TIP: Save time by using a store-bought rotisserie chicken. Simply shred the breast meat. Then save the bones in your freezer to create a nourishing chicken stock. Looking for a kick of heat? Toss the shredded chicken with 1 teaspoon of chili powder before adding to the soup.

SPRING CHICKEN SOUP

PREP TIME: 10 minutes   **COOK TIME:** 35 minutes

The phrase "spring chicken" evokes a sense of energetic youth with some bounce in your step. We can't guarantee that's what this soup will do for you, but it is chock-full of some of the best spring produce. If you're cooking it later in the year, use frozen or canned produce in place of ingredients that aren't at the peak of freshness.

2 tablespoons olive oil

1 large onion, diced

1 large carrot, sliced

2 celery stalks, sliced

2 garlic cloves, minced

Salt

Freshly ground
   black pepper

4 boneless, skinless
   chicken thighs (about
   1 pound)

2 medium parsnips,
   peeled and chopped

2 cups halved cherry
   tomatoes

6 cups low-sodium
   chicken stock

4 cups baby spinach

1 small bunch Swiss
   chard or rainbow chard,
   stemmed and chopped

1 cup green peas

10 thin asparagus spears,
   trimmed and cut to
   1-inch pieces

1. In a large stockpot or Dutch oven, heat the olive oil over medium-high heat. Add the onion, carrot, and celery and sauté until the onion is translucent, about 5 minutes. Add the garlic and season with salt and pepper; then cook about 1 minute more.

2. Add the chicken, parsnips, and tomatoes; then cover with the stock. Bring to a boil; then reduce the heat and simmer, uncovered, for about 20 minutes.

3. Use a slotted spoon to remove the chicken thighs. Coarsely chop the cooked chicken; then return it to the pot. Add the spinach, Swiss chard, peas, and asparagus and simmer about 5 minutes more.

4. Season with salt and pepper to taste. Serve immediately.

INGREDIENT TIP: Asparagus is a perennial favorite for the springtime, but the size of the stalks varies. The ends are woody and fibrous, so remove those before cooking, regardless of the thickness of each spear. If using thick spears, add to the pot earlier to allow them to cook to a crisp-tender texture. If using thinner spears, add them later in the cooking process.

SOUTHWESTERN TURKEY SOUP

PREP TIME: 15 minutes   **COOK TIME:** 20 minutes

This hearty, health-supportive soup can be put together in minutes. Feel free to add or remove ingredients as you like; if you don't like beans or corn, you can omit those. But if you can have it all, this robust soup will likely become a family favorite.

1 tablespoon olive oil

1 pound ground turkey

1 zucchini, sliced

2 garlic cloves, minced

1 teaspoon kosher salt

1 teaspoon chipotle powder

½ teaspoon ground cumin

¼ teaspoon freshly ground black pepper

4 cups low-sodium chicken stock or vegetable broth

1 (15-ounce) can black beans, drained and rinsed

1 (14.5-ounce) can diced fire-roasted tomatoes (optional)

1 cup frozen corn (optional)

OPTIONAL TOPPINGS

Greek yogurt

Scallions, both white and green parts, finely chopped

Fresh cilantro, chopped

1. In a Dutch oven, heat the olive oil over high heat.

2. Add the turkey and cook, stirring frequently, until browned, about 5 minutes.

3. Add the zucchini, garlic, salt, chipotle powder, cumin, and pepper and sauté until tender, about 5 minutes.

4. Add the stock, black beans, fire-roasted tomatoes and their juices (if using), and corn (if using).

5. Bring to a boil; then reduce to a simmer and simmer to heat through and combine the flavors, about 10 minutes.

6. Ladle into bowls and serve with the toppings (if using).

WHITE CHICKEN CHILI

PREP TIME: 5 minutes   COOK TIME: 25 minutes

This chili is made with hearty beans, tender chicken, and a rich and creamy broth with zero dairy. Using mashed beans lends this soup creaminess. It is an easy technique you can also use to thicken sauces.

2 tablespoons olive oil

1 large onion, diced

1 jalapeño pepper, seeded and finely diced

4 garlic cloves, minced

1 (7-ounce) can green chiles, drained

1 tablespoon ground cumin

1 teaspoon dried oregano

¼ teaspoon red pepper flakes

2 (15-ounce) cans cannellini beans, drained and rinsed, divided

6 cups low-sodium chicken stock, divided

Juice of 1 lime

4 cups shredded cooked chicken

Salt

Freshly ground black pepper

½ cup chopped fresh cilantro, for garnish

1. In a large pot, heat the olive oil over medium-high heat. Add the onion and jalapeño and cook for 5 to 7 minutes, until the onion is translucent and the jalapeño is tender. Add the garlic and cook until fragrant, 1 to 2 minutes.

2. Add the green chiles, cumin, oregano, and red pepper flakes. Stir to combine.

3. In a blender or food processor, blend 1 cup of the beans with ¼ cup of stock until smooth and creamy.

4. Add the blended bean mixture, the remaining 5¾ cups of stock, and the lime juice to the pot. Bring to a gentle boil and cook for 10 minutes. Add the remaining whole beans and chicken. Reduce to a simmer and cook for an additional 5 minutes until the chicken and beans are warmed through.

5. Season with salt and pepper to taste. Garnish with the cilantro.

INGREDIENT TIP: Canned green chiles come with different spice levels. Choose the spice level that you would enjoy best.

Provençal
Pistou Soup
(page 82)

CHAPTER FOUR

VEGETABLE SOUPS

POTATO-LEEK SOUP

PREP TIME: 5 minutes **COOK TIME:** 30 minutes

The simplicity of this soup is amazing. It's a subtle reminder that, sometimes, the simplest things are the most flavorful. The famed French chef Louis Diat, who trained in Paris kitchens before moving to New York City, claims he "invented" vichyssoise in 1917, basing it on his mother's recipe for *soupe bonne femme*.

2 tablespoons
  unsalted butter

1 sweet onion, diced

3 leeks, white part only,
  diced and washed well

1 garlic clove, mashed

8 ounces Yukon Gold
  potatoes, peeled
  and sliced

4 cups low-sodium
  chicken stock or water

Salt

Ground white pepper

1 cup heavy (whipping)
  cream (optional)

1. In a large saucepan, melt the butter over low heat. Add the onion, leeks, and garlic. Cook, covered, until the vegetables are very tender, about 10 minutes.

2. Add the potatoes and stock and bring to a boil over high heat. Reduce the heat to low and simmer until the potatoes are tender, 10 to 15 minutes. Season with salt and pepper to taste.

3. Stir in the cream (if using), heat through, about 4 minutes, and serve.

INGREDIENT TIP: Leeks can be really dirty and require soaking to remove the dirt before cooking. Cut the white part from the leeks and halve lengthwise. Submerge in water and thoroughly clean between each layer before draining and chopping.

VARIATION: To make this a creamy soup, puree in a blender and serve hot, garnishing with a spoonful of sour cream and a sprinkling of chopped fresh chives. Serve it chilled and it's vichyssoise.

CREAM OF BROCCOLI SOUP WITH LEMON AND CHILI

PREP TIME: 5 minutes   COOK TIME: 20 minutes

Broccoli is the star of the show in this tasty, comforting gluten-free soup. For maximum nutrition, chop the broccoli about an hour ahead of time. This allows for the production of a heat-resistant phytochemical called sulforaphane, a potent cancer fighter. Don't have time to spare? Buy pre-chopped bags of broccoli at the supermarket.

2 tablespoons olive oil

2 broccoli
  heads, chopped

¼ teaspoon red
  pepper flakes

4 garlic cloves, smashed

8 cups low-sodium
  chicken stock

Zest and juice of
  1 lemon, divided

1 cup plain yogurt or
  plant-based yogurt

Salt

1. In a large pot, heat the olive oil over medium heat. Add the broccoli and sauté for 2 to 3 minutes, until it begins to turn bright green. Add the red pepper flakes and garlic. Cook for 30 seconds, until just fragrant.

2. Stir in the chicken stock, half the lemon zest, and half the lemon juice. Bring the soup to a simmer and cook for 15 minutes, or until the broccoli is tender. Remove the soup from the heat.

3. Using an immersion blender, puree the soup until mostly smooth, retaining some texture.

4. Add the yogurt and the remaining lemon zest and blend again. Taste and season with salt and the remaining lemon juice, if necessary. Serve immediately or cover and refrigerate for up to 3 days.

FRENCH ONION SOUP

PREP TIME: 10 minutes   COOK TIME: 2 hours 45 minutes

French onion soup is perhaps the most iconic and well traveled of all French dishes. The real flavor comes from the deep caramelization of the onions, so be sure to spend the time to deepen their color before making the soup.

3 tablespoons unsalted butter

2 bacon strips, diced

4 sweet onions (2 to 2½ pounds total), sliced paper thin

4 garlic cloves, mashed

1 tablespoon all-purpose flour (optional)

10 cups low-sodium chicken stock, beef stock, or water

1 cup red wine

1 thyme sprig

1 bay leaf

1 baguette, sliced

6 ounces Emmental cheese, grated

2 ounces mozzarella cheese, grated

1. In a large Dutch oven or heavy stockpot, melt the butter over medium heat until foamy. Add the bacon and cook, stirring often, until lightly browned, about 4 minutes. Add the onions and garlic and cook, stirring often, until the onions are soft and lightly browned, about 30 minutes.

2. Reduce the heat to low and cook, stirring frequently, until the onions are very brown, about 1½ hours. Adjust the heat even lower, if necessary, to keep them from burning. The sweetness and richness of flavor come from this step.

3. Sprinkle the onions with the flour (if using; this addition gives the soup a bit more depth and body). Add the stock, wine, thyme, and bay leaf and simmer until golden brown with a rich taste, about 30 minutes.

4. While the soup is simmering, preheat the oven to 350°F.

5. Place the baguette slices directly on the oven racks and bake until lightly browned, about 15 minutes. Remove from the oven and preheat the broiler.

6. In a small bowl, combine the cheeses. To serve, ladle the soup into 8 ovenproof bowls, and then top each with 2 bread slices and ¼ cup of the cheese. Working in batches if necessary, set the bowls on a baking sheet and broil until the cheese is golden brown, about 5 minutes.

LENTIL AND RED PEPPER SOUP

PREP TIME: 15 minutes   COOK TIME: 30 minutes

This is an easy, healthy soup; adding feta cheese at the end infuses brightness into the earthy flavors. There are two kinds of lentil soup: the type that's a thick, porridge-like soup and the type where the lentils retain their basic shape so you can see each individual one. If you like the second type, reduce the simmering time or use green lentils instead of red.

2 tablespoons olive oil

2 red bell peppers, coarsely chopped

1 onion, coarsely chopped

1¾ cups shredded carrots

2 tomatoes on the vine, coarsely chopped

5 garlic cloves, coarsely chopped

Salt

Freshly ground black pepper

8 cups low-sodium chicken stock

2 cups red lentils

1 teaspoon dried oregano

½ teaspoon dried rosemary

Juice of ½ lemon

½ cup crumbled feta cheese, for serving

1. In a large stockpot, heat the olive oil over medium-high heat. Add the bell peppers, onion, carrots, tomatoes, and garlic and stir to combine. Season with salt and pepper and cook for 5 to 7 minutes, until the onion is soft.

2. Add the stock, lentils, oregano, and rosemary and bring to a boil. Reduce the heat to low and simmer for 20 minutes, or until the lentils are tender.

3. Using an immersion blender or a food processor, puree the soup until smooth. Stir in the lemon juice. Taste and adjust the seasonings, if desired.

4. Serve topped with the feta.

PREP TIP: Don't worry too much about the size of the chop for the bell peppers, onion, tomatoes, and garlic—you'll be blending the soup before serving.

SPLIT PEA SOUP

PREP TIME: 10 minutes   **COOK TIME:** 1 hour 40 minutes

Traditionally, split pea soup is made by simmering a ham hock. This vegan twist results in a smoky and flavorful soup utilizing anti-inflammatory herbs and spices, like garam masala, an Indian spice blend. Garam masala traditionally consists of coriander, cumin, cardamom, cloves, black pepper, and nutmeg. If you don't have this blend on hand, make your own following the instructions in the Ingredient Tip.

2 tablespoons olive oil	1 teaspoon	6 cups low-sodium
2 medium	ground cumin	vegetable broth
onions, chopped	½ teaspoon dried basil	1 cup water
2 carrots, chopped	½ teaspoon	Salt
3 celery stalks, chopped	garam masala	Freshly ground
2 cups green split peas	2 bay leaves	black pepper

1. In a large pot, heat the olive oil over medium-high heat. Add the onions, carrots, and celery. Sauté for 5 to 7 minutes, until the onions are translucent and the vegetables are tender.

2. Stir in the split peas, cumin, basil, garam masala, and bay leaves.

3. Add the broth and stir to combine. Bring to a boil; then reduce to a low simmer. Cover and cook for 1½ hours, stirring every 30 minutes, until the peas are tender.

4. Stir and adjust the consistency by adding ½ cup of water at a time.

5. Remove the bay leaves. Season with salt and pepper to taste.

INGREDIENT TIP: No garam masala? Create your own spice blend with a combination of 1 tablespoon of ground cumin, 1½ teaspoons of ground coriander, 1½ teaspoons of ground cardamom, 1½ teaspoons of freshly ground black pepper, 1 teaspoon of cinnamon, ¼ teaspoon of ground cloves, and ¼ teaspoon of ground nutmeg. Place the mix in an airtight container, and store in a cool, dry place.

TUSCAN WHITE BEAN SOUP

PREP TIME: 10 minutes   **COOK TIME:** 30 minutes

This hearty and healthy rustic soup is sure to impress and incredibly easy to make. Pearled couscous is toasted semolina flour shaped into small balls. If you can't find it, simply use a different grain that you like, or omit it and double the amount of beans. The cooking time may vary depending on the time needed to cook the substituted grain.

2 tablespoons olive oil

1 large onion,
   finely chopped

3 medium carrots,
   finely chopped

3 celery stalks,
   finely chopped

4 garlic cloves, minced

1 tablespoon
   tomato paste

2 teaspoons
   dried oregano

1 teaspoon dried basil

8 cups low-sodium
   vegetable broth

1 (15-ounce) can petite
   diced tomatoes

1 cup pearl couscous

1 (3-inch) Parmesan rind

1 (15-ounce) can
   cannellini beans,
   drained and rinsed

3 cups shredded
   stemmed Lacinato kale

Salt

Freshly ground
   black pepper

Shredded Parmesan
   cheese, for serving

1. In large pot, heat the olive oil over medium-high heat. Add the onion, carrots, and celery. Sauté until the onion is translucent and the vegetables are tender, 5 to 7 minutes. Add the garlic and cook until fragrant, 1 to 2 minutes.

2. Add the tomato paste, oregano, and basil. Stir to coat the vegetables.

3. Add the broth, tomatoes and their juices, couscous, and Parmesan rind. Bring to a boil; then reduce to a simmer and cook for 15 to 20 minutes, until the couscous is tender.

4. Remove the Parmesan rind, if it hasn't disintegrated. Add the beans and kale. Cook until the kale has wilted. Season with salt and pepper to taste.

5. Pour the soup into bowls and top with shredded Parmesan cheese.

VARIATION: Lacinato or dinosaur kale is a fun ingredient to cook with, but if you can't find it, look for other varieties of kale, or swap it out for Swiss chard or rainbow chard.

CARROT-GINGER SOUP

PREP TIME: 10 minutes   **COOK TIME:** 20 minutes

This soup allows the flavor of the carrots to shine and gets an added anti-inflammatory flavor boost from the ginger. This makes a great light lunch when paired with a salad or sandwich, or add silken tofu to the soup before pureeing to add protein for a more filling meal on its own.

2 tablespoons olive oil

2 pounds carrots, chopped

4 cups low-sodium chicken stock

2 teaspoons ground ginger

1 cup milk

1 tablespoon fennel seeds or fresh chopped mint, for garnish

1. In a large stockpot, heat the olive oil over medium-high heat until shimmering.

2. Cook the carrots for 5 minutes, until they are just about to begin caramelizing.

3. Add the chicken stock and ginger and bring the soup to a low boil.

4. Simmer the soup for 10 minutes, until the carrots are tender.

5. Remove the soup from the heat, add the milk, and stir.

6. Working in four small batches, transfer the soup to a blender. For each batch, cover tightly and puree on high or on the smoothie setting for 30 to 60 seconds. Transfer the pureed soup to a serving bowl.

7. Serve each bowl of soup with a garnish of fennel seeds or mint.

VARIATION: This recipe can be made vegan by using vegetable stock instead of chicken stock and nondairy milk. For a creamier texture, you can use 1 cup of coconut cream or silken tofu in place of the nondairy milk.

CREAMY AVOCADO SOUP WITH ORANGE-PEPPER SALSA

PREP TIME: 15 minutes

The superfood ingredients in this flavorful soup work synergistically. Red bell pepper and oranges are excellent sources of essential vitamins for your health. And, according to multiple studies, avocado can quadruple the absorption of the beneficial nutrients found in fruits and vegetables. It's a wonderfully flavorful soup you can feel great about eating.

FOR THE SALSA

1 red bell pepper, diced

1 orange, peeled and segmented

½ cup finely diced fresh cilantro

½ jalapeño pepper, seeded and minced

Juice of 1 lime

FOR THE SOUP

2 cups water

3 large ripe avocados, halved and pitted

1 cucumber, peeled and coarsely chopped

1 celery stalk, coarsely chopped

½ cup coarsely chopped fresh cilantro

Juice of 1 lime

1 teaspoon ground coriander

1 teaspoon kosher salt

½ teaspoon grated orange zest

TO MAKE THE SALSA

1. In a medium bowl, combine the red bell pepper, orange segments and accumulated juices, cilantro, jalapeño, and lime juice. Gently toss to mix. Set aside.

TO MAKE THE SOUP

2. In a blender, combine the water, avocado, cucumber, celery, cilantro, lime juice, coriander, salt, and orange zest. Puree until completely smooth.

3. Divide the soup among serving bowls and top with the salsa. This soup is best enjoyed immediately.

SERVES 4 to 8

DAIRY-FREE, 45 MINUTES OR LESS

HOT AND SOUR SOUP

PREP TIME: 20 minutes   COOK TIME: 10 minutes

A traditional Chinese New Year soup, this recipe combines the heat of hot sesame oil with the acidity of vinegar and the characteristic numbing effect of Sichuan peppercorns.

9 cups low-sodium
  chicken stock, divided
¼ cup rice vinegar
1 teaspoon hot sesame oil
1 teaspoon ground
  Sichuan peppercorns
1 ounce sliced dried
  shiitake or tree ear
  mushrooms

12 canned
  bamboo shoots
2 tablespoons cornstarch
8 ounces ground pork
1 (16-ounce) package
  firm tofu, cut into
  ½-inch cubes

4 large eggs, beaten
1 bunch (6 to 8) scallions,
  both green and white
  parts, cut into ¼-inch
  pieces, for garnish

1. In a 4-quart pot, combine 8 cups of stock with the vinegar and sesame oil and bring to a boil over high heat. Stir in the peppercorns, dried mushrooms, and bamboo shoots.

2. In a medium bowl, whisk together the cornstarch and the remaining 1 cup of stock; then stir the mixture into the stock for about 2 minutes, until it thickens.

3. Crumble the pork into the broth. Then add the tofu and cook for about 5 minutes, until the pork is cooked through.

4. While gently stirring the stock, drizzle in the eggs, forming shreds.

5. Remove the soup from the heat and sprinkle with the scallions just before serving.

RUSSIAN BORSCHT

PREP TIME: 15 minutes   **COOK TIME:** 1 hour 10 minutes

Borscht is actually a Ukrainian recipe, but it is very popular in Russia as well as communities across the United States. It differs from many vegetable-based soups because the vegetables are sautéed separately instead of cooking in the broth itself. If stew meat isn't available, you can use ground beef in its place.

1 tablespoon olive oil

1 pound beef stew meat, trimmed and cut into small cubes

6 cups low-sodium beef stock

2 large carrots

2 large beets, peeled

1 large russet potato, peeled

2 celery stalks, sliced thin

8 ounces shredded green cabbage (about ¼ medium cabbage head)

¼ cup tomato paste

2 garlic cloves, minced

1 tablespoon white vinegar

Salt

Freshly ground black pepper

¼ cup chopped fresh parsley or dill, for garnish

1 cup sour cream, for garnish

1. In a heavy-bottomed nonstick skillet, heat the olive oil over medium-high heat. Add the stew meat and brown on all sides, about 5 minutes.

2. Meanwhile, in a large stockpot or Dutch oven, bring the stock to a low simmer.

3. Once the beef is browned, transfer to the stock and simmer, stirring occasionally, for 1 hour (30 minutes if using ground beef.).

4. In the meantime, shred the carrots, beets, and potato. Add the shredded vegetables, celery, and cabbage to the skillet, scraping the bottom of the pan to combine the flavors from browning the beef. Sauté for 15 minutes, until all the vegetables appear wilted and softened. Add the tomato paste and garlic. Transfer 1 cup of the hot stock to the skillet and simmer for 3 to 5 minutes.

5. Stir in the vinegar; then carefully transfer the vegetables to the stockpot with the beef. Season with salt and pepper to taste; then serve in bowls garnished with fresh parsley. Top with the sour cream and serve.

GAZPACHO

PREP TIME: 10 minutes, plus 2 hours to chill

A classic of Spanish cuisine, gazpacho originated in the southern region of Andalusia. It is the quintessential summer soup not only because it's served chilled but also because all of the seasonal ingredients are at the peak of ripeness. This recipe can be made up to 2 days in advance. As it sits in the refrigerator, the flavors will deepen.

2 large beefsteak toma-
  toes, divided
1 English cucum-
  ber, divided
1 medium red
  onion, divided

3 cups low-sodium
  tomato juice
1 (15-ounce) jar roasted
  red peppers, drained
1 bunch cilantro, chopped
  (about ½ cup)

⅓ cup red wine vinegar
¼ cup olive oil
Hot sauce
Salt
Freshly ground
  black pepper

1. Chop one tomato, half the cucumber, and half the onion into 1-inch pieces.

2. Transfer to a blender with the tomato juice, roasted red peppers, cilantro, vinegar, olive oil, and hot sauce (to taste). Puree until smooth. Transfer to a bowl and set aside.

3. Seed the remaining tomato and chop into a small dice. Also dice the remaining cucumber and red onion. Stir into the soup.

4. Season with salt and pepper to taste. Refrigerate for at least 2 hours before serving.

5. Serve chilled. Garnish with diced cucumber and cilantro leaves as desired.

INGREDIENT TIP: English cucumbers, also known as seedless cucumbers, are found wrapped in plastic at the grocery store. Why? Because they have a more delicate skin that is not covered in wax. If you are not using an English cucumber, then simply scoop out the seeds of the conventional cucumber, which tend to be bitter.

CREAMY TOMATO-BASIL SOUP

PREP TIME: 10 minutes   **COOK TIME:** 45 minutes

There's really nothing more comforting than a steaming-hot bowl of tomato soup. Canned tomatoes work great instead of fresh, not only for convenience but because they are packed in peak season, meaning they're perfectly ripe. Canned tomatoes are loaded with powerful antioxidants, some of which have been found to be more absorbable by the body in their cooked form.

2 tablespoons olive oil

1 large Vidalia onion, chopped

3 garlic cloves, minced

2 tablespoons all-purpose flour

1 (28-ounce) can whole peeled tomatoes

3 cups low-sodium chicken stock

1 cup milk

¼ cup chopped fresh basil

1 teaspoon sugar

Salt

Freshly ground black pepper

Shredded Parmesan cheese (optional)

1. In a large pot, heat the olive oil over medium-high heat. Add the onion and sauté until translucent, 5 to 7 minutes. Then add the garlic and cook until fragrant, 1 to 2 minutes.

2. Add the flour and stir to coat the onion and garlic.

3. Add the tomatoes and their juices and the stock. Bring to a simmer while stirring to make sure all the ingredients are incorporated and the flour is not sticking to the bottom of the pan. Reduce the heat to low, cover, and simmer for 30 minutes.

4. Turn off the heat. Stir in the milk, basil, and sugar to combine.

5. Using an immersion blender, blend the soup until creamy. Alternatively, in small batches using a high-speed blender, blend the soup until smooth.

6. Season with salt and pepper to taste. Top with Parmesan cheese (if using) and a fresh basil leaf.

INGREDIENT TIP: When your soup is simmering, throw in a rind of Parmesan cheese. The rind will soften, and the flavors of the cheese will infuse the dish. Remove any undissolved rind when you're ready to blend the soup.

MISO SOUP

PREP TIME: **10 minutes**   COOK TIME: **5 minutes**

You've likely enjoyed miso soup out at a restaurant, but it's surprisingly easy to make at home—this recipe uses just five ingredients. Miso, a fermented paste traditionally made from soybeans and salt, simmers to create a rich, savory broth. Find it in the refrigerated section of the grocery store near the tofu.

6 cups water

3 (2-inch) pieces kombu

⅓ cup white miso

8 ounces silken tofu, drained, cut into small cubes

4 scallions, both white and green parts, finely chopped

1. In a large pot, combine the water and kombu over medium heat. Remove the kombu just as the water starts to come to a boil. Then turn down to a simmer.

2. Place the miso in a small bowl. Scoop out about ½ cup of broth and pour it over the miso. Whisk together until the miso has dissolved in the water and no lumps remain. Add the miso to the simmering broth. Stir to combine.

3. Reduce the heat to low and add the tofu to the miso broth. Heat through just enough to warm the tofu, 1 to 2 minutes.

4. Just before serving, stir in the scallions. Serve warm.

INGREDIENT TIP: Kombu is dried seaweed, most often used in soups and broths to add an umami flavor. For extra depth of flavor, add bonito (dried fish flakes), commonly found in Asian markets. (The soup will no longer be vegan, however.)

STORAGE TIP: Cool, cover, and store leftovers in the refrigerator for 3 to 4 days.

MINESTRONE

PREP TIME: 10 minutes   COOK TIME: 35 minutes

This one-pot minestrone soup is full of vegetables, pasta, and an incredible tomato base. It makes a satisfying dinner on a cool fall day. It's quick, it's healthy, and it's perfect for dunking using some crusty bread. Minestrone was traditionally made to use up leftover vegetables, so feel free to use any vegetables and greens you have on hand. It's also delicious served with a dollop of pesto on top.

2 tablespoons olive oil

1 large onion, diced

5 garlic cloves, minced

3 celery stalks, diced

2 large carrots, diced

8 ounces green beans, trimmed and cut into ½-inch pieces

1 teaspoon dried oregano

1 teaspoon dried basil

1 teaspoon dried parsley

8 cups low-sodium vegetable broth

1 (28-ounce) can diced tomatoes, drained

1 (14-ounce) can crushed tomatoes

1 (15-ounce) can dark red kidney beans, drained and rinsed

1 cup small shells pasta (conchiglie) or macaroni

Salt

Freshly ground black pepper

Grated Parmesan cheese (optional)

1. In a large pot, heat the olive oil over medium-high heat. Add the onion and cook until translucent, about 3 minutes. Add the garlic and cook for 1 minute or until fragrant.

2. Add the celery and carrots, stir to combine, and cook until they begin to soften, about 5 minutes.

3. Stir in the green beans, oregano, basil, and parsley, and cook for 3 minutes.

4. Add the broth, diced tomatoes, and crushed tomatoes to the pot. Bring to a boil; then reduce to a simmer for 10 minutes.

5. Stir in the kidney beans and pasta and simmer for an additional 10 minutes, until the pasta and vegetables are tender.

6. Season with salt and pepper to taste. Top with Parmesan cheese or pesto, (if using).

ROASTED BUTTERNUT SQUASH SOUP

PREP TIME: 15 minutes   **COOK TIME:** 1 hour

This simple roasted vegetable soup is a perfect way to celebrate the autumn harvest. The butternut squash adds a slightly sweet, nutty flavor and is loaded with antioxidants and vitamins.

1 butternut squash, quartered and seeded

1 small onion, halved

2 tablespoons olive oil

¼ teaspoon kosher salt

1 rosemary sprig

3 cups low-sodium chicken stock

1 celery stalk, cut into 1-inch pieces

1 garlic clove, lightly smashed

Freshly ground black pepper

1. Preheat the oven to 400°F.

2. On a rimmed baking sheet, rub the squash and onion with the olive oil. Sprinkle with the salt. Spread everything out in a single layer and add the rosemary sprig.

3. Roast for 1 hour, until the squash is tender and starting to brown. Set aside to rest for 5 minutes. Discard the rosemary.

4. Meanwhile, when the squash is nearly done, in a small saucepan, combine the stock, celery, and garlic, and heat over medium-low heat for about 15 minutes, until the celery is tender.

5. Using a spoon, scrape the squash flesh out of the skin and into a blender. Add the roasted onion, cooked celery and garlic, and a few ladles of stock. Remove the center cap from the blender lid to allow steam to escape, hold a kitchen towel over the hole, and blend until smooth. Add more stock until you get the consistency you desire. Season to taste with salt and pepper.

PROVENÇAL PISTOU SOUP

PREP TIME: 20 minutes   **COOK TIME:** 1 hour

This soup transports you to the South of France with a punch of pure pesto (known there as pistou) stirred in. Serve it with a baguette and a glass of wine and bring yourself to Provence and those lovely lavender fields.

FOR THE SOUP

1¼ cups dry white beans

4 quarts vegetable stock or water

1 teaspoon sea salt, divided

1 bay leaf

2 tablespoons extra-virgin olive oil

1 yellow onion, peeled and diced

½ red bell pepper, diced

2 carrots, diced

1 teaspoon dried thyme

1 small yellow squash, diced

4 tomatoes, diced

4 small zucchini, thinly sliced

4 small red potatoes, quartered

½ pound fresh green beans, stemmed and sliced into 1-inch pieces

1 cup small pasta like mini shells or macaroni

½ teaspoon freshly ground black pepper

1 cup packed chopped Swiss chard

FOR THE PISTOU

2 cups fresh basil leaves, packed

½ cup extra-virgin olive oil, plus 2 tablespoons

4 garlic cloves

4-ounces grated Parmesan cheese

TO MAKE THE SOUP

1. Place the beans in a medium bowl and cover them with about 3 inches of water. Let soak at room temperature overnight.

2. Drain and place the beans in a large stockpot with the water, ½ teaspoon salt, and the bay leaf. Bring to a boil over high heat, reduce the heat to low, cover, and simmer until beans are al dente, about 45 minutes.

3. While the beans cook, heat the oil in a large skillet over medium-high heat and sauté the onion, pepper, carrot, and the remaining salt until softened and translucent, about 5 minutes. Add the thyme and the squash and cook until the squash begins to soften, about 5 minutes more.

4. Add the onion and squash mixture to the cooked beans and water. Add the tomatoes, zucchini, green beans, pasta, and pepper. Cook until the pasta is al dente, about 15 minutes. Stir in the chard and remove from heat.

TO MAKE THE PISTOU

5. Place the basil, oil, and garlic in a food processor or blender and process until smooth. Spoon the mixture into a bowl and fold in the cheese.

6. Ladle the soup into warm soup bowls and garnish with a large spoonful of the pistou.

PREP TIP: The soup can be made ahead, but do not make the bright green pistou until just before serving.

Crab Bisque
(page 87)

CHAPTER FIVE

SEAFOOD SOUPS, BISQUES, AND CHOWDERS

MANHATTAN CLAM CHOWDER

PREP TIME: 15 minutes   **COOK TIME:** 25 minutes

Homemade chowder is surprisingly easy to make and tastes so much better than canned versions. Bacon adds a subtle smoky element that really builds on the flavor, but you can leave it out if you prefer. Serve this soup with some crusty bread and a dash or two of hot sauce for an extra kick of flavor.

4 bacon slices, chopped	1 (14.5-ounce) can diced	1 (10-ounce) can baby
1 onion, diced	fire-roasted tomatoes	clams, drained
2 celery stalks, diced	2 red potatoes, diced	Juice of 1 lemon
2 carrots, diced	1 cup low-sodium	Salt
4 garlic cloves, minced	chicken stock	Freshly ground
1 teaspoon dried oregano		black pepper

1. In a Dutch oven, fry the bacon for 5 minutes over high heat, or until crispy. Turn the heat to low.

2. Add the onion, celery, carrots, garlic, and oregano. Cook for 5 minutes, stirring occasionally, until the vegetables begin to soften.

3. Add the tomatoes and their juices, potatoes, chicken stock, and clams. Bring the chowder to a simmer. Cook for about 15 minutes until the potatoes and carrots are soft.

4. Remove from the heat and stir in the lemon juice. Season to taste with salt and pepper.

INGREDIENT TIP: Baby clams are smaller and more tender than chopped clams, although you can use those if you prefer.

CRAB BISQUE

PREP TIME: 10 minutes   COOK TIME: 15 minutes

Crab and mint is a classic flavor combination and is exquisite in this creamy soup. You can leave out the Parmesan if you wish, but it gives the soup an added layer of flavor and texture. Another tasty way to serve this is to float several croutons in the soup, added just before serving.

4 tablespoons unsalted butter

¼ cup all-purpose flour or white rice flour

6 cups seafood stock

1 mint sprig

Zest of 1 lemon

1 cup heavy (whipping) cream

1½ pounds lump crabmeat

1¼ cups finely grated Parmesan cheese

Salt

Freshly ground black pepper

1. In a large pot, cook the butter and flour over medium heat for 2 minutes, whisking constantly until bubbling and thick.

2. Pour in the seafood stock, whisking to distribute the roux.

3. Add the mint sprig and lemon zest. Simmer for 5 minutes to thicken.

4. Add the cream and simmer for 5 more minutes; then stir in the crab and simmer until heated through. Remove the pot from the heat and allow the soup to cool briefly.

5. Remove the mint sprig and stir in the Parmesan cheese. Season with salt and pepper. Garnish with fresh herbs of your choice, such as mint leaves, parsley, or dill, to serve.

MEDITERRANEAN SEAFOOD STEW

PREP TIME: 10 minutes
COOK TIME: 8 to 10 hours, plus 10 to 15 minutes to cook the seafood

This stew gives a strong nod to ratatouille, a Provençal dish of slow-cooked eggplant, zucchini, tomatoes, and herbs. The seafood cooks in a flash at the end. Serve with a loaf of crusty French bread.

1 red onion, halved and thinly sliced from stem to roots

1 eggplant, cut into 1-inch pieces

2 medium zucchini, cut into 1-inch pieces

1 (15-ounce) can plum tomatoes, hand torn

½ cup coarsely chopped fresh herbs, such as parsley, basil, thyme, and rosemary

4 garlic cloves, minced

¼ cup olive oil

Salt

Freshly ground black pepper

2 pounds clams

1 pound jumbo shrimp

1 lemon, cut into wedges

1. In a slow cooker, toss the onion, eggplant, zucchini, tomatoes, herbs, and garlic with the olive oil. Season generously with salt and pepper. Stir; then cover and cook on low for 8 to 10 hours.

2. Just before you're ready to serve, scrub the clams. Peel the shrimp. Nestle them into the vegetables, but don't completely bury them. Cover, increase the heat to high, and continue cooking for 10 to 15 minutes, or until the shrimp are opaque and the clams have opened. Discard any clams that have not opened after 15 minutes.

3. Turn off the slow cooker. Divide the stew among serving bowls.

4. Serve the stew with the lemon wedges.

VARIATION: To cook on the stove top, in a large, heavy pot, heat 2 tablespoons of the olive oil over medium heat until shimmering. Add the onion and cook, stirring, until beginning to brown, about 6 minutes. Add the eggplant and zucchini and cook for 2 to 3 minutes, until starting to brown. Add the tomatoes, herbs, garlic, and remaining 2 tablespoons of oil and stir to combine. Season with salt and pepper. Bring to a simmer and cook over medium-low heat, covered, for 45 to 60 minutes, or until the vegetables are very soft and beginning to break apart. Increase the heat to medium-high and add the clams. Cover the pot and cook for 5 to 10 minutes, or until the clams have opened. Stir in the shrimp and simmer for 3 to 5 minutes, or until done.

SERVES 4 to 6

DAIRY-FREE, 45 MINUTES OR LESS

BOUILLABAISSE

PREP TIME: **10 minutes**   COOK TIME: **20 minutes**

This Provençal stew is loaded with seafood and the distinctive flavor combination from the fennel, orange zest, and saffron. While it may seem intimidating to make this classic French dish, it's actually really easy to make and cooks in one pot, making cleanup all the easier.

2 tablespoons olive oil

1 large yellow onion, sliced

2 garlic cloves, smashed

⅓ cup finely chopped fennel fronds

2 teaspoons grated orange zest

Salt

Freshly ground black pepper

¼ teaspoon saffron threads

6 cups seafood or vegetable stock

1 (14-ounce) can diced tomatoes

8 ounces cod, cut into 1- to 2-inch chunks

8 ounces halibut, cut into 1- to 2-inch chunks

8 ounces medium shrimp, peeled and deveined

10 clams, soaked in cold water for 10 minutes, drained, and scrubbed

10 mussels, scrubbed, beards removed

1 cup chopped fresh parsley

Crusty artisan bread (optional), for serving

1. In a large, heavy soup pot, heat the olive oil over medium-high heat. Add the onion, garlic, fennel, and orange zest.

2. Season with salt and pepper and add the saffron. Cook for 2 to 3 minutes, until fragrant. Add the seafood stock and tomatoes. Bring to a boil.

3. Once boiling, reduce the heat and bring to a simmer. Add the cod and halibut. Cook for 7 to 8 minutes.

4. Next, add the shrimp, clams, and mussels. Cook for another 5 to 6 minutes, until the clam and mussel shells have opened, the shrimp turns pink, and the fish flakes easily with a fork. Discard any mussels or clams that haven't opened.

5. Turn off the heat, add the fresh parsley, and stir. Ladle the stew into bowls and serve warm with slices of crusty bread (if using).

GREEN CURRY SHRIMP NOODLE SOUP

PREP TIME: 10 minutes   COOK TIME: 15 minutes

Sweet, spicy, tangy green curry serves as a delicious backdrop for whatever healthy vegetables are in season. Full-fat coconut milk creates a creamy, rich soup, but you can substitute light if you prefer. Mirin and orange juice bring a pleasant balance of sweetness and acidity to the dish. If you can't find mirin, use white wine.

2 tablespoons canola oil

1 small onion, halved and thinly sliced

4 large garlic cloves, minced

1 tablespoon minced peeled fresh ginger

1 lemongrass stalk, bottom 3 inches removed and halved, remaining 12 inches or so discarded

¼ cup Thai green curry paste

¼ cup mirin

¼ cup freshly squeezed orange juice

8 cups fish stock

1 (15-ounce) can full-fat coconut milk

8 ounces green beans, trimmed and cut into 2-inch pieces

1 pound jumbo shrimp, peeled and deveined

8 ounces brown rice noodles, pre-soaked in hot water for 10 minutes

1 cup coarsely chopped fresh Thai basil, or Italian basil, for garnish

2 limes, cut into wedges, for garnish

1. In a large pot, heat the canola oil over medium heat. Add the onion, garlic, ginger, and lemongrass. Cook for about 5 minutes, until the vegetables begin to soften, being careful not to burn the garlic.

2. Stir in the curry paste, mirin, and orange juice. Simmer the mixture for 2 to 3 minutes, until some of the liquid has evaporated.

3. Add the fish stock and coconut milk and bring the soup to a simmer.

4. Add the green beans and shrimp. Cook for about 3 minutes, or until the shrimp are cooked through (pink and opaque) and the green beans are bright green. Remove and discard the lemongrass pieces.

5. Drain and divide the rice noodles among serving bowls. Ladle the curry over the noodles in each bowl and garnish with basil and lime wedges.

PRESSURE COOKER CIOPPINO

PREP TIME: 5 minutes   **PRESSURE COOK TIME: 7 minutes**   **RELEASE TIME: 10 minutes**

This recipe uses an electric pressure cooker and swaps shellfish, like mussels, for frozen shrimp and scallops to make prep a breeze. It's great to add a pinch of saffron to the broth—it goes so well with tomatoes and makes this seafood stew extra special. This stew is even tastier the next day; make it ahead and gently reheat until warmed through.

1 tablespoon olive oil

2 celery stalks, minced

1 onion, minced

1 green bell pepper, minced

2 garlic cloves, thinly sliced

4 cups marinara sauce

1¼ cups low-sodium fish stock

1 teaspoon dried oregano

Generous pinch saffron threads

1 pound frozen medium shrimp

1 pound frozen scallops

2 tablespoons chopped fresh parsley

Salt

Freshly ground black pepper

1. On the pressure cooker, select Sauté. Pour in the olive oil to heat.

2. Add the celery, onion, bell pepper, and garlic. Cook for 3 to 4 minutes to soften.

3. Stir in the marinara, fish stock, oregano, and saffron threads. Add the shrimp and scallops. Lock the lid in place and set the cooker to High pressure for 3 minutes.

4. When the cook time ends, let the pressure release naturally for 10 minutes; then manually release any remaining pressure.

5. Carefully remove the lid and top the cioppino with the parsley. Season to taste with salt and pepper.

VARIATION: To make this on the stove top, in a large pot, heat the olive oil over medium-high heat. Sauté the celery, onion, bell pepper, and garlic for 3 to 4 minutes to soften. Add the marinara, stock, oregano and saffron and stir to combine. Bring to a simmer, then add the shrimp and scallops and cook, covered, for 10 to 15 minutes, until the shrimp and scallops are cooked through and the flavors meld. Season with salt and pepper and garnish with parsley.

WILD SALMON AND SOBA HOT POT

PREP TIME: 10 minutes   COOK TIME: 20 minutes

This tasty soup features salmon, healthy buckwheat noodles, and tender spring vegetables in a flavorful dashi stock. Choose wild fish for the most nutrition and the lowest environmental impact.

8 ounces soba

8 cups dashi stock
  (4 teaspoons dashi
  powder dissolved in
  8 cups hot water)

¼ cup mirin

2 tablespoons soy sauce

1 carrot, julienned

4 ounces snow
  peas, trimmed

½ bunch tender aspar-
  agus, tough woody
  ends trimmed, remain-
  ing spears cut into
  2-inch pieces

1 pound wild salmon fillet

1. Bring a large pot of salted water to a boil over high heat. Add the soba and cook according to the package directions, about 8 minutes. Drain and divide the noodles among serving bowls.

2. While the soba cook, in a large pot over medium-low heat, heat the dashi stock. Add the mirin and soy sauce.

3. Stir in the carrot, snow peas, and asparagus. Add the salmon on top of the vegetables. Cover the pot and gently simmer (at the barest simmer) for 8 minutes, or until the vegetables are tender and the fish flakes easily with a fork. Divide the fish and vegetables among the serving bowls, over the noodles, and ladle the broth into each.

INGREDIENT TIP: Keep a clean pair of pliers in the kitchen to remove fish bones. Place your fingertips on either side of the bone so the flesh of the fish doesn't tear. Grasp the tip of the bone with the pliers and gently pull to remove.

FISH AND TOMATO RICE SOUP

PREP TIME: **10 minutes**   COOK TIME: **35 minutes**

Soups often do well with canned tomatoes, but this soup is extra good during tomato season. There's something wonderful about pints of fresh heirloom cherry tomatoes, sweet and bursting off the vine, seeds squirting everywhere. If they aren't yet in season, you can use a can of diced tomatoes in their place.

1 tablespoon olive oil

1 small onion, finely diced

2 carrots, finely diced

1 celery stalk, finely diced

4 garlic cloves, minced

½ teaspoon red
  pepper flakes

1 teaspoon anchovy paste
  (optional)

2 cups coarsely chopped
  cherry tomatoes

6 cups low-sodium
  chicken stock or
  vegetable broth

2 cups long-grain
  white rice

1½ pounds firm whitefish,
  such as cod, cut into
  2-inch pieces

½ cup chopped fresh
  cilantro

¼ cup freshly squeezed
  lime juice

Lime wedges, for serving

1. In a large pot, heat the olive oil over medium-low heat. Add the onion, carrots, and celery and cook for 5 minutes, or until the vegetables begin to soften.

2. Add the garlic, red pepper flakes, and anchovy paste (if using) and cook for 1 minute.

3. Add the cherry tomatoes and cook for another 5 minutes, or until the tomatoes burst.

4. Pour in the stock and bring to a simmer. Add the rice, cover, and cook for 15 minutes; the rice will not yet be cooked through.

5. Add the fish, cover the pot, and cook for 5 to 10 minutes or until the fish is cooked through.

6. Stir in the cilantro and lime juice. Serve immediately with the lime wedges.

STORAGE TIP: Cool, cover, and store leftovers in the refrigerator for up to 2 days.

NEW ENGLAND CLAM CHOWDER

PREP TIME: **15 minutes**   COOK TIME: **1 hour**

Clam chowder is a warming winter soup with a creamy base. Heavy cream makes the soup extra rich, and seafood stock and bacon provide its layered flavors. Croutons provide a great contrast of texture and flavor and are the perfect topping for this comforting soup.

4 bacon slices,
    coarsely chopped

4 celery stalks,
    finely diced

1 onion, finely diced

4 to 6 garlic
    cloves, peeled

Salt

4 cups seafood stock

1 thyme sprig

4 potatoes, peeled
    and diced

1 cup heavy
    (whipping) cream

2 (6-ounce) cans
    clams, drained and
    coarsely chopped

Handful croutons
    (optional)

1. In a large pot, cook the bacon over medium-low heat for 10 to 15 minutes, until it has rendered its fat and is nice and crispy. Transfer it to a paper towel.

2. Add the celery, onion, and garlic to the bacon fat in the pot and season with salt. Cook for 10 minutes until the vegetables are soft.

3. Add the stock and thyme sprig and bring to a simmer. Add the potatoes and cook for 25 minutes, until tender.

4. Remove the thyme and discard. Remove about 2 cups of the stock and potatoes and puree until smooth. Return the puree to the pot and stir in the cream. Bring to a simmer and cook for 5 minutes until thick.

5. Stir in the clams and cook just until heated through. Ladle the soup into individual serving bowls and garnish with the cooked bacon and croutons (if using).

VARIATION: If you want a dairy-free clam chowder, you're in luck. This recipe works beautifully with coconut milk or coconut cream. To make the chowder without bacon, simply use butter or olive oil to cook the vegetables and stir in ¼ teaspoon of liquid smoke seasoning during the last 2 minutes of cooking.

SHRIMP AND TORTELLINI SOUP

PREP TIME: 10 minutes   COOK TIME: 20 minutes

Tortellini soup is a northern Italian recipe traditionally served as a first course during holiday meals, especially at Christmas. The addition of the protein from shrimp takes this soup from starter to main course.

2 celery stalks, chopped

1 carrot, chopped

1 shallot, finely diced

2 garlic cloves, thinly sliced

1 (1-inch) piece fresh red chile, seeded and minced

1 thyme sprig

1 (2-inch) strip lemon peel

1 teaspoon kosher salt

¼ teaspoon freshly ground black pepper

Pinch ground nutmeg

1 cup water

¼ cup dry white wine (optional)

8 cups low-sodium chicken stock

12 ounces large shrimp, peeled and deveined

20 ounces fresh cheese tortellini

2 tablespoons grated Parmesan or Romano cheese, for garnish

1. In a soup pot, combine the celery, carrot, shallot, garlic, chile, thyme, lemon peel, salt, pepper, and nutmeg. Add the water and wine (if using), cover, and bring to boil over medium-high heat. Boil for about 5 minutes, until the vegetables are soft.

2. Add the chicken stock, cover, and return to a boil.

3. Add the shrimp and continue to boil, uncovered, for 1 minute, until the shrimp start to turn pink.

4. Add the tortellini and continue to boil for 3 to 4 minutes, or according to the package directions, until cooked through.

5. Remove and discard the thyme sprig and lemon peel.

6. Serve sprinkled with the Parmesan.

MEASUREMENT CONVERSIONS

VOLUME EQUIVALENTS	U.S. STANDARD	U.S. STANDARD (OUNCES)	METRIC (APPROXIMATE)
LIQUID	2 tablespoons	1 fl. oz.	30 mL
	¼ cup	2 fl. oz.	60 mL
	½ cup	4 fl. oz.	120 mL
	1 cup	8 fl. oz.	240 mL
	1½ cups	12 fl. oz.	355 mL
	2 cups or 1 pint	16 fl. oz.	475 mL
	4 cups or 1 quart	32 fl. oz.	1 L
	1 gallon	128 fl. oz.	4 L
DRY	⅛ teaspoon	–	0.5 mL
	¼ teaspoon	–	1 mL
	½ teaspoon	–	2 mL
	¾ teaspoon	–	4 mL
	1 teaspoon	–	5 mL
	1 tablespoon	–	15 mL
	¼ cup	–	59 mL
	⅓ cup	–	79 mL
	½ cup	–	118 mL
	⅔ cup	–	156 mL
	¾ cup	–	177 mL
	1 cup	–	235 mL
	2 cups or 1 pint	–	475 mL
	3 cups	–	700 mL
	4 cups or 1 quart	–	1 L
	½ gallon	–	2 L
	1 gallon	–	4 L

OVEN TEMPERATURES

FAHRENHEIT	CELSIUS (APPROXIMATE)
250°F	120°C
300°F	150°C
325°F	165°C
350°F	180°C
375°F	190°C
400°F	200°C
425°F	220°C
450°F	230°C

WEIGHT EQUIVALENTS

U.S. STANDARD	METRIC (APPROXIMATE)
½ ounce	15 g
1 ounce	30 g
2 ounces	60 g
4 ounces	115 g
8 ounces	225 g
12 ounces	340 g
16 ounces or 1 pound	455 g

INDEX

ABOUT THE AUTHOR

 **Janet A. Zimmerman** is an award-winning food writer and the author of 10 previous cookbooks. She taught avocational cooking classes for 20 years and has been writing about food for almost as long. Previously from San Francisco, she now lives in Atlanta with her partner, Dave.